entirely by sea and the transport of building materials from the mainland and those recovered from the demolition of old palaces was carried out by a myriad of boats and rafts. But later, little by little as the bridges were built (there are over 400 today), it became possible to move on foot from one island to another without going on the water, and work could proceed more rapidly. Venice gradually developed in a harmonius and functional way along the largest waterways which meandered between the islands. The merchants' houses, bright and simple as they were, were built side by side in a line overlooking the smooth water, with an opening at the front (the «riva») for unloading the merchandise, a porch to give shelter and access to the storerooms (the «fondaci»). The progressive growth in the stature of the merchants, corresponded not only with their settlement in the heart of the city and the spread of a prestigious and elegant urban centre, but also with development of the political influence wielded by this class which gave a considerable impulse to the rise of the Venetian Republic. Also the political centre of the city began to take shape. A Palace of Justice and a «Palazzo Comune» (Town Hall), then a large ceremonial piazza or square, and the «Cappella Ducale» (Ducal Chapel) were placed beside the first Doge's Palace which had been built next to the shipping dock. Work was started on the «Cappella Ducale» in 829. The Basilica of St. Mark, known originally as the Cappella Ducale or the Ducal Chapel because it was adjacent to the Ducal Palace is emblematic of Venice's cultural and spiritual position astride the Eastern and Western civilizations. The typically Byzantine structure with its Greek cross plan and five large domes, had no precedent on the Italian peninsula; but it was to St. Mark that it was dedicated, a saint belonging to Latin religious history and who became the symbol of Venice and its desire for independence from Constantinople. Trade with the East, source of riches and prestige, became ever more flourishing. Venice, which had grown out of the need for a refuge, succeeded in overcoming the natural restrictions of its lagoon configuration and conquered the open sea. In the year one thousand the Republic already ruled the Adriatic and East Mediterranean coasts from Dalmatia to Puglia and to the Greek islands, and was in an advantageous commercial relationship with Byzantium. The ships of the Republic left Venice loaded with wool and silk, timber and metals and returned carrying precious stones, silks, spices, grain, wines, and sugar to the European markets. Thus Venice established itself as the greatest maritime power in Europe. Right along the Adriatic and the Aegean as far as the Dardanelles and the Sea of Marmara, the Venetians created a network of maritime ports and settlements. They pushed into Asia Minor and had economic ties with Egypt from 1200. Marco Polo crossed the borders of the known world and brought back riches and extraordinary tales from China. The political prestige of Venice reached its height during the dogate of Enrico Dandolo when, taking part in the IV Crusade, he conquered Constantinople in 1204. Although the dominion over Constantinople, shared with the French, was of short duration, favourable commercial relationships continued afterwards, enabling Venice to maintain its extraordinary economic prosperity. Economic prosperity was the basis of the aristocratic power of the Republic whose constitutional continuity was surprising when compared with the political instability which characterized the Italian peninsula after the fall of the Roman Empire. A consolidated constitution already existed in the XII century with the figure of the Doge flanked by aristocratic organizations

which prevented the Dogate being transformed into a monarchy. The Minor Council, the High Council, the Procurators of St. Mark, the Council of the «Pregadi», to mention a few, were all part of the complex political organism which ruled the Republic. And its constitutional stability was certainly a valuable card in the tireless struggle which Venice had to pursue against Genoa for supremacy of the East Mediterranean. The conflict knew no respite during the 13th and 14th centuries until in 1380 Venice wrestled Chioggia from the Genoese invaders and finally wiped them out. Construction began on the new Ducal Palace in 1340. The Gothic style which had developed successfully in Europe, was adopted by Venice but with an unusual and original stylistic difference. The Ducal Palace is a fine example of this Venetian Gothic or 'decorated Gothic' finished as it is with typical Venetian chiaro-scuro decorations on the two main fronts. In the 15th century the attention of Venice, which was already mistress of the Adriatic and the Eastern markets, turned to the mainland. The Italian and North European markets were extremely difficult to reach because of customs duties which were imposed by the neighbouring powers. In fifty years of conflict and economic investment, Venice conquered Brescia, Bergamo, part of Trentino, Udine, the Friulis and Polesine, thus opening a way to the West, the North and the South. Venice was a power and a centre not only of economic exchange: it was the goal of men of culture, scholars and artists from every part of the peninsula and it welcomed every cultural contribution the mainland could offer. In fact towards the end of the 15th century the Renaissance, which was born in Tuscany, spread farther afield and found its way to Venice where it made still further changes in the appearance of the city. The art of Donatello and of Leon Battista Alberti arrived in Venice with their pupils and followers among whom were Pietro Lombardo and Mauro Coducci. The scenario of Venetian architecture, its sense of colour and of light, found new expressive stimuli in the spirit of the Renaissance. The façades of the palaces were covered with coloured marbles, fine carving and sculpture, always without losing the plastic grace which is their great characteristic. The School of St. John the Evangelist, the School of St. Mark, the Church of the Miracles, Vendramin Calergi Palace, the Corner-Spinelli Palace, the Great Clock Tower, are illustrious examples of this period of Venetian architecture which was to continue to develop with a stylistic and expressive refinement which even in the sixteenth century was to know moments of extraordinary splendour. In 1538 Sansovino designed the Library to complete the Piazzetta of San Marco, and then the Ca' Corner. Along with architecture, Venetian painting also enjoyed its golden moment with the work of such artists as Titian, Tintoretto, Giorgione, Jacopo Bassano, and Paolo Veronese. It was only between the sixteenth and seventeenth centuries that the slow political decline of Venice began. Occupied on one side in defending their commercial bases in the East against the Turks who were opposing them at sea, and involved, on the other, in the wars of an unstable mainland continually being upset by attempts at political rearrangement by various European powers, Venice became weakened both militarily and economically. In 1571 the Venetians won a brilliant victory against the Turks at Lepanto but it proved to be no more than a flash of light in the ever more gloomy picture of exhausting battles at sea and progressive relinquishment of Venice's hold over its commercial outposts. However, the city continued to grow with constant determination and full creativity.

VENICE

CIVILISATION, ART AND HISTORY

Editions KINA ITALIA

History

Trains, cars and coaches rush rapidly across the long bridge that separates Venice from Mestre, from the motorway, and from the noise of the mainland. Already between the sea and the sky the slow lazy flight of a seagull contrasts with our hurried course towards the lagoon city. Then, punctually, the enchantment engulfs us again and again: Venice receives the visitors, and as a majestic and self-assured host, puts a stop to all this hurrying and draws him into the gentle rhythm of the amphibian city. One may decide to walk along the calli, those long narrow lanes, go up and down the bridges, cross the campi and campielli (the squares and smaller squares) or take the waterway and cross the city by steamboat along the Grand Canal, between the multicoloured scenario of the most beautiful palaces in the world, all of which overlook its waters. Always, the reality exceeds the expectation. Everyone in this city built on 120 tiny islands talks of the extraordinary power of the ancient marine republic, of the strength, the enterprise of its inhabitants and of the splendid civilization of which they were the artificers.

Emigrating during the 5th century from various parts of the Veneto Region such as Aquileia, Oderzo, Altino, Monselice, to escape from the invading Huns and later, from the Longobards, they took refuge in the lagoon then inhabited only by a few fishermen, salt gatherers and hunters in the swamps. From a modest appendage of the Romano-Byzantine province of Venezia-Istria, governed first by a military tribunal from Byzantium, the Venice on the lagoon was destined to become an autonomous centre and, eventually, the political and cultural connecting link between West and East. Miserable and inhospitable though it must have appeared to its first inhabitants, the lagoon proved a safe haven, impenetrable to anyone who had not a perfect knowledge of the varied and continually changing morphology. Thanks to this fact the people who arrived there in search of a temporary refuge found a place where they could continue to live undisturbed. Thus the lagoon centres of Cittanova, Eraclea, and Torcello were born, the latter a mercantile port soon to become the main junction for lagoon traffic, the administrative centre and episcopal seat. In the meantime Venice's subordination to the Exarch of Ravenna, the representative of the Empire, was lessening. After the first doges of imperial nomination, in 726, perhaps following the Italian revolt against the Emperor Leo III, for the first time Venice elected its doge autonomously: He was Orso Ipato, the first of a series who were to reign for over a millenium. Venice grew as a political entity and, more slowly, also in its urban structure. The ducal seat which was first transferred from Cittanova to Malamocco, was established in 811 on the island of Rivoalto. Rialto looks over the waters of the Grand Canal and it soon became clear that this waterway would become the most important artery of the maritime traffic of the city, the principal connection between the sea and terrafirma, while on its two banks the splendid habitations of the merchants were built to make it also the heart of the urban centre. Already grown rich from trade with the East, the merchant and seafaring classes moved to the city, leaving the wealthy and busy mercantile port of Torcello. And in the heart of Venice, on the banks of what is still a slow, muddy river, the most spectacular urban nucleus in the world began to take shape. Originally, circulation took place

Baldassare Longhena designed the Salute Church in the Dorsoduro district, the Seminary and the Customs station, creating a very considerable change in the urban scene at St. Mark's, the object of admiration but also of disapproval of the separation of the Church from the urban context in which it had been born. Begun in the 1600's, also by Longhena, the Pesaro and Rezzonico Palaces were to become the most magnificent residences on the Grand Canal. But the eighteenth century was the most fertile century for outstanding artistic personalities, a century of recovery. Among all the arts it was certainly painting which enjoyed the most intense spirit of innovation. From the impetuous and dramatic temperament of Tiepolo, an artist much in demand at all the Courts in Europe, to the satyrical vain of Longhi who depicted the customs of contemporary society, and the happy contemplation of Guardi and Canaletto in their «views» of Venice, Venetian painting found original expression and continued to be a point of reference for European art during the following centuries. The Churches of St. Stae, of the Jesuits, of the Pietà and of the Fava and, among civil buildings, Palazzo Grassi and Palazzo Pisani are all examples of the architecture of this time while music also had a particularly happy period with the artistic production of Benedetto Marcello, Vivaldi and Boccherini. Unfortunately, the vitality and perfection of the artistic production was at least equalled by the weakness and lack of direction in the political field. The political class of the aristocratic Venetian government was living, as if frozen, in a European context continually disturbed by new upheavals and the anarchical blast of the French Revolution. Venice had lost its dominion of the sea and over the eastern ports. On terrafirma it became involved in ever more disastrous undertakings and in 1797 it was conquered by Napoleon and lost even its own liberty. Foreign troops landed at St. Mark's basin, an event without precedent in the history of Venice. A meeting of the High Council was called for the last time and decreed the end of the Republic. For almost a century Venice, deprived of all military and political strength, was at the mercy of the historical events which regarded the neighbouring powers. First it was annexed to the Kingdom of Italy, proclaimed by Napoleon, and later to the Lombard-Veneto Kingdom under the dominion of Austria, which it had to put up with until 1866 except for the revolutionary attempts led by Daniele Manin in 1848-49. After the Austro-Prussian War Venice, whose political destiny was put to popular vote, became definitively Italian. The cultural and artistic revival of the city was gradual, but it was definite. With the institution of the Biennial of Modern Art and the International Film Festival Venice, already possessor of a rich artistic patrimony from the past, became an international point of reference also for contemporary art and culture. The one really serious problem nowadays is that of the safety of the city which is threatened by the breakdown of the hydro-geological equilibrium caused by a slow but progressive sinking with respect to the level of the water; the pollution caused by petro-chemical establishments in the nearby industrial centres; and vibration caused by motor driven means of transport. The combined political forces of Venice and several international organizations are trying to rescue Venice from a destiny of death; endeavouring to preserve its beauty; to halt the tendency of its population to leave the city; and to reinforce that natural instinct for life which Venice has demonstrated throughout its history and which emanates from the lively beauty of its architecture and from its artistic treasures.

The Principal Basilicas

A tour of the great basilicas of Venice gives the visitor a rich and multiform picture not only of the spiritual, but of the political and artistic life of the Republic. From the Basilica of St. Mark with its oriental style domes; the Basilica of the Salute with its great white bulk reflected majestically in the waters of St. Mark's basin; the Gothic Basilica of the Frari, simple and evocative with its pure lines; and the Church of Sts. John and Paul (or of St. Zanipolo as the Venetians call it) which houses numerous tombs of doges and military leaders of the Republic. It is said that St. Mark's is an open book on the history of Venice because its architecture, the stratification of decorative elements; the composite and narrative style employed in the stories reproduced in the splendid gilded mosaics; the spoils of war including many things from churches destroyed on the mainland and now preserved within its walls, are all kept together in St. Mark's as if in a single great fantastic record of the remote past of the Republic. The Basilica, which for several centuries was the ducal chapel, has witnessed the celebration of all the most important moments in the History of the Serenissima, from the departure on a Crusade to the drama of the plague which afflicted the city. It was here in 1630, in the presence of the Patriarch Tiepolo and Doge Contarini, that vows were offered to the Madonna imploring her to free the City of Venice from the terrible pestilence. The Basilica of the Salute (Health), built just beyond St. Mark's Basin, bears testimony to that dramatic moment and to the gratitude felt towards the Virgin for the gracious liberation from the scourge. Built by Baldassare Longhena, it is a stylistically unique and important example of the Venetian seventeenth century. The Basilica of the Frari, or more correctly, of Santa Maria Gloriosa of the Frari, is an example of the Gothic style with great harmony and beauty, and contains an artistic patrimony of outstanding importance. Its most precious jewel is undoubtedly Titian's altarpiece of the *Assumption*, which Canova described as «the most beautiful picture in the world». Lastly, the Church of Sts. John and Paul can be considered the Pantheon of the Glories of the Republic: the tombs of numerous doges and military leaders, evidence of the political and military life of Venice are also extremely interesting examples of funerary art. The tomb of Doge Andrea Vendramini, XV century, is looked upon as the real masterpiece of them all. These churches will be discussed more exhaustively on later pages. But there are of course many more churches in Venice which are of interest for their history, architecture and artistic patrimonies. To mention a few: the Church of *St. Zachariah*, founded in the IX Century by Doge Giustiniano Partecipazio and rebuilt several times until it acquired its present form with a most beautiful Gothic façade: *St. Stephen*, XIV century, which also has frequently been restored and has a magnificent great doorway; the Church of the *Madonna dell'Orto*, an interesting example of the period of transition from Romanesque to Gothic and to the Renaissance; and finally the Church of the *Redeemer*, a masterpiece of religious architecture by Palladio, that also, like the Salute Church, was built as a votive offer in thanks for the liberation from the plague in 1576.

St. Mark's Basilica

In a splendid architectural scenario, St. Mark's dominates the square which Napoleon called «more the drawing-room of the world» and the heart of Venice; an open book on the spiritual and political history, rich and multiform artistic testimony to those events which saw the Republic as the central pivot of the Eastern and Western worlds and their respective cultures. According to legend, when the evangelist St. Mark arrived at the islands in the lagoon, he dreamt that the angel said to him «Here you will find peace, my evangelist». Thus, when in the year 828 the saint's body was taken from the Moham-medons in Alexandria in Egypt to Venice by two merchants, the people's exultation on receiving it was the crowning of a spiritual duty performed, a sign that the well-deserved protection written into his destiny had been fulfilled. The following year Doge Giustiniano Partecipazio ordered the construction of the temple destined to receive the saint's remains. It was consecrated in 832 as the «Ducal Chapel» and so it remained for several centuries becoming, only in 1807, the Cathedral of Venice. Thus it was first a State Church

1) The majestic facade of St. Mark's basilica with the famous cupolas. On the balcony overlooking the five lower arcades is the famous old quadriga.
2) Christ in Gloria and Final Judgment
3) Detail of balcony

under the Dukedom with an autonomous clergy independent of the Patriarch. Right from the beginning St. Mark's was the place of thanksgiving and exultation, of hope and of pain, it was the site chosen for the ritual ceremonies for all the most important historical happenings in the Republic: the IV Crusade set out from St. Mark's after the standards had received the blessing of Venice; prayers were said in St. Mark's for the protection of the naval troops on their departure to rescue Chioggia from the Genoese invaders; and St. Mark's was the meeting place for the reconciliation between Frederick Barbarossa and Pope Alexander III. But the Basilica was also a monument to richly creative expression, successful and multiform. In it, centuries of art and generations of artists both famous and unknown have left evidence of the most varied styles, from Byzantine and Romanesque to Gothic and Renaissance. And, far from appearing as a hybrid mixture of unrelated and discordant works, the Basilica is a miraculous and evocative choral composition in which the refinements of the more cultured arts mingle happily with the more ingenuous expressions of

1) View of St. Mark's square
2) Northern façade facing Piazzetta dei Leoncini
3) The Four Moors
4) The Sansovino loggia
5) The Sansovino loggia: detail

popular phantasy. According to numerous historians the Basilica was originally built in the traditional form of the paleo Christian, Ravennate or pre-Romanesque temples. So, presumably it had a nave and two aisles, one or two apses with the relative crypts and an arcade or narthex in front. The Venetians had probably decorated it with architectural elements removed from abandoned buildings on the mainland but it is not known if it was already covered with mosaics as it is now, or with frescoes. The fire which broke out in the nearby Ducal Palace after a revolt of the people in 976, so completely destroyed it that it had to be rebuilt, as it was in the following two years. But it was only in 1063 that Doge Contarini began construction of the present grandiose and magnificent Basilica. Venice had already become rich and powerful and its political and economic importance was to be expressed to the full in the Ducal Chapel. Thus St. Mark's was rebuilt for the third time in its present form, that of a Greek Cross, with four domes on the arms and a fifth in the middle: a typically Byzantine design, due to an unknown architect, possibly a Greek. It was a sign of the cultural opening of Venice towards the East but with the addition of several original elements of its own in the interpretation and embellishment of the Church. Work

1) Clock tower and horse from the quadriga
2) View from St. Mark's basilica
3) The clock with the signs of the Zodiac

Lunette on the so-called San Alipio door: mosaic depicting the transfer of the body of St. Mark into the basilica.

14

continued on and in the new basilica until the sixteenth century. The Venetians reused some of the materials and parts of the previous basilica: window and door posts, capitals, transennae, some of which were replaced in their original positions and some set into the walls as a testimony to the past and as an historical record. From time to time new additions were made; marbles of every type and colour, columns of every style and size (there are more than 500 today), Romanesque bas-reliefs and Venetian sculptures, Romanesque, Gothic, and Byzantine capitals, all, as has been said, in an extraordinarily harmonious combination made particularly sumptuous by the mosaics with their golden backgrounds which cover part of the façade and, in the interior, all the vaulting and the domes and much of the upper walls. St. Mark's fills one side of the square named after it, its unusual façade has two orders of arches, five on ground level and the five above set slightly back. Under the five lower arches, separated by groups of multicoloured columns, are five doorways each of which is decorated with fine bas-reliefs of episodes in religious history (the marriage of Cana, the Epiphany, Christ and the Apostles, etc., in the St. Alipio doorway) or scenes describing the daily life of the city («Occupations» representing the principal occupations of the people of Venice, on the third doorway). The arches overlooking the narrow terrace above the lower line of arches, are surmounted by Gothic decorations with statues, foliage and cusps. The central arch, wider than the others like the corresponding one below, is

1) St. Clement's door, in bronze damascened in gold, silver and multicolored enamels

2) Mosaic from the 13th century located in the vault of the right chancel depicting the transfer of the body of the Evangelist to our lagoons

3) Detail of the atrium, 13th century: Noah is releasing the dove from the Ark after the flood

closed by a large glass window through which the interior of the basilica receives light and which also serves as a background for the four famous bronze horses. This splendid example of Greco-Alexandrine art, attributed by some to Lysippus, formed part of the plunder from the sacking of Constantinople by the Venetians who conquered the city in 1204. The fine domes emerge from behind the façade and terminate in the Eastern style lantern with the shining crosses crosslet above. One passes to the interior of the Basilica through first the atrium with its magnificent marble mosaic paving and the splendid mosaics made by Venetian craftsmen in the XIII century which represent biblical stories, from the Creation to the Flight into Egypt. The interior, a grandiose and magnificent series of domes and arches, contains a rich collection of artistic treasures worthy of a lengthy and detailed examination. The four arms of the Greek cross which represent the main structure support the domes which rest on large barrel vaults above pilasters. That of the presbytery apart, the other three arms

1) Iconostasis: Gothic structure of the 14th century
2) The dance of Salomè: detail
3) Interior of St. Mark's basilica seen from the central nave with the Byzantine cross that descends from the Pentecost cupola

Pages 20-21: the Pala d'Oro (Golden Altar-Piece)

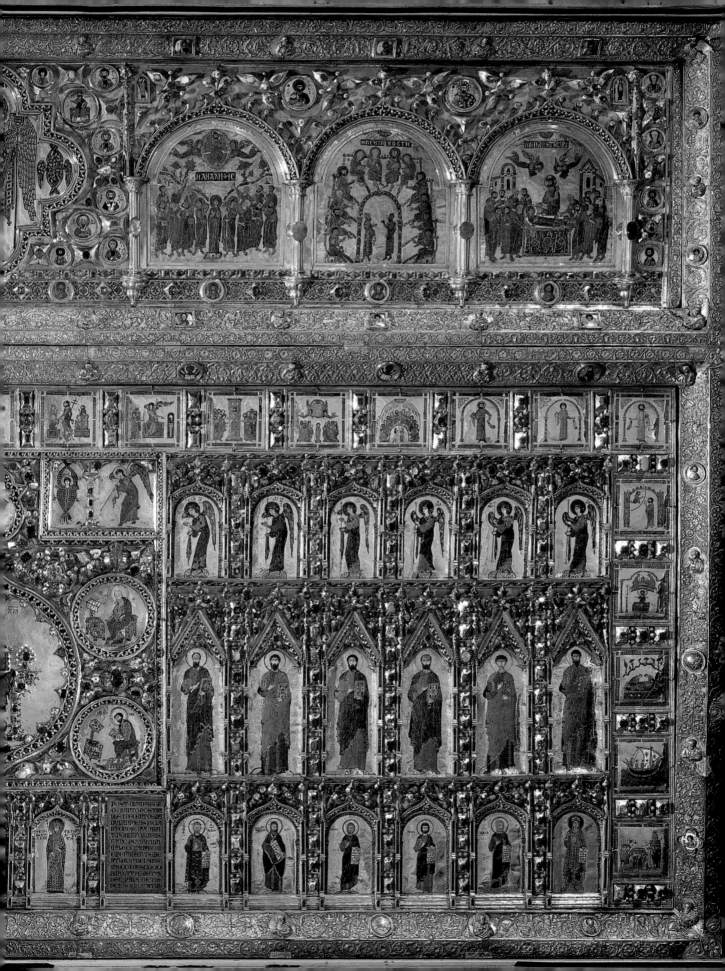

are each divided into a nave and two aisles by pillars which are joined by arches on columns which support the galleries. The body of St. Mark, kept at one time in the XI century crypt, is now under the table of the High Altar. A ciborium supported on four alabaster columns richly carved with stories from the Bible, covers and gives imposing grandeur to the altar. The *Pala d'Oro* (the Gold Altarpiece), thickly encrusted with gems and enamels is composed of several parts which were made over a period from the X to the XIV century and is among the most precious treasures in existence. Among the various inner chapels, dedicated to St. Clement, St. Isadore, St. Theodore, St. Peter, the Madonna dei Maseoli and the Madonna Nicopeia, the last one is of particular historical interest. Nicopeia means victory and is believed to have been carried, with other sacred images, at the head of the army of the Byzantine Emperors from whom it may have been seized in 1204 with the rest of the plunder. She is the traditional Protectress or Patroness of Venice and is the most venerated image in the Basilica. But wha makes St. Mark's the 'Basilica of Gold' and bestows the greatest magnificence upon it, is the splendid mosaic mantle which covers an area of over 4000 metres of roof. Begun presumably during the dogate of Domenico Selvo (1071-1084) when the apse was decorated with the four evangelists, the mosaics of St. Mark's are an extraordinary example of anonymous art. At a

later date, in the fifteenth and sixteenth centuries, famous painters such as Jacopo Bellini, Paolo Uccello, the Mantegna, Titian and Tintoretto were to design the cartoons for mosaics which were then carried out by craftsmen. But before that time, this art of Byzantine and Ravennate origin was entrusted entirely to the creative genius and executive ability of masters who have remained anonymous, who chose the subjects, designed the pictures and executed the mosaic work. The art of mosaic, of which notable examples are also to be found in other Venetian churches, was a natural expression of the artistic ability of a craftsman in glasswork who had furnaces at Murano. The tiles made of glass paste could be produced in a vast variety of colours from Vermilion to emerald green. Used with a background of tiles faced with gold leaf, these colours acquired light and brilliance. Inspiration for the subjects came from various sources: the Byzantine tradition from such examples as the mosaics in the Church of the Apostles in Constantinople and, for the mosaics in the atrium, other references

1) St. Mark heals a man possessed by demons
2) An Angel appears in St. Mark's dreams and commands him to go to Alexandria
3) Mosaics in the atrium: Genesis cupola

come from the Cotton Bible. These latter which have already been mentioned, depict stories from the Old Testament and serve as an historical introduction to the sacred themes in the interior of the Basilica. Here, following a narrative thread represented by the idea of the Church «promised», «functional», and «triumphant», we have the Prophets, the Apostles, the Ascension and Paradise portrayed on the larger domes. On the walls and the minor domes other parallel stories complete the narrative with episodes from the life of Christ and the Virgin, the Passion of Jesus, the life of St. Mark with the famous episode of the theft of the body, the lives of St. Peter and other saints. All the artistic styles, recognizable from the stratification and superimposition of architectural elements are equally recognizable in the mosaics, where the Byzantine tradition, but also Romanesque art, decorated Gothic and the Renaissance are all represented. Thus, as many love to define it, St. Mark's Basilica is a casket which jealously conserves in its custody, the trembling, palpitating expression of the spirituality and of the history of Venice.

1) The Virgin Nicopeia: this is the most venerated image in the basilica
2) Two doves facing each other: a portion of the mosaic carpet near the entry to the Treasury
3-4) Details of floor

Pages 26-27: the quadriga

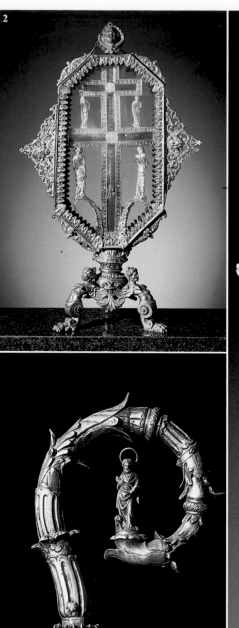

1) *Sardonyx ampulla from the 3rd century*
2) *Reliquary for the cross of the king of Flanders*
3) *Reliquary for the arm of St. George*
4) *Pastoral cross staff*
5) *Incense burner or processional lamp in the form of a building with cupolas*

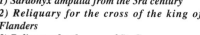

5

Basilica della Salute

The majestic construction of the Basilica di Santa Maria della Salute (or St. Mary of Health) is on the Trinità Island in the Dorsoduro ward, and faces towards St. Mark's Basin. It was during the terrible plague from which some thousands died in Venice in 1630 that a special votive service was held in St. Mark's imploring the Madonna to free the city from the pestilence. Then in 1631 Baldassare Longhena was commissioned to build the Basilica in thanks to the Virgin for bringing about the end of the epidemic and in 1633, after the difficult work of reinforcing the ground had been completed the Basilica was finally begun. The construction of the Basilica was finished in 1653 while completion of the minor domes and other decorative elements proceeded for several decades. Longhena took his inspiration for the building based on a central plan, from the architecture of Bramante and Palladio. He designed the church with an octagonal plan culminating in an enormous semispherical dome, flanked at a later date by a second, smaller cupola above the presbytery. An impressive polygonal stone stairway leads to the entrance

1) The Basilica della Salute seen from the Grand Canal
2) Basilica della Salute and the Jewish quarter
3) Detail of the basilica as seen from above
4) General view of the floor

3

4

doorway in the central façade which has the appearance of a triumphal arch. The door, with two leaves, is made of oak and faced with sheets of bronzed copper. Three lateral façades correspond to six chapels which surround the wide central well of the church. Fifteen modillions or trusses in concentric strata emphasize the majesty of the dome and underline the chromatic effect of the white stone which is used also for the principal façades and for the numerous statues of angels, saints and Marian figures of the Old Testament. Very few of these statues are of easy attribution and most are the work of totally unknown artists. A particularly beautiful one is that of the Archangel Michael striking Lucifer, in the first façade on the left, and St. John the Baptist, perhaps by Ruer, at the second entrance from the right. The Madonna and Child over the tympanum above the entrance, represents the central point of the iconographical theme which dominates the entire church both inside and out: the Glorification of Mary. The interior of the Basilica, nobly constructed, luminous and solemn, consists of a wide central well surrounded by composite orders of columns on high plinths and powerful pillars which support the great dome, a good 60 metres

from the floor to the topmost point of the lantern. The floor, an extraordinary piece of work, is a mosaic made of polychrome marble in concentric circles with outer bands in a multicoloured geometrical design giving an optical illusion effect, while a ring of thirty-two roses surrounding the middle circle are a symbolic reference to the Marian Rosary. The marble statues which adorn the altar represent the cleansing of the city of the pestilence. In the centre is an image of the Madonna della Salute (the Madonna of Health) which was brought here from the Cathedral of Candia in 1670. Around the High Altar six chapels open towards the centre of the Church, they are all dedicated to a mystery of the Virgin, except the Altar of St. Anthony. The altarpieces by Luca Giordano, Pietro Liberi and Titian are valuable parts of the rich patrimony of the Basilica. The sacristy, in fact, contains twelve works by Titian which were brought here from the Island of Santo Spirito, they represent various periods in his artistic development. There are other works by Palma the Younger, Padovanino, and the famous canvas painted by Tintoretto in 1561 of the Marriage of Cana, and intended for the refectory of the Fathers Bearers of the Cross.

1) The main altar, by J. Le Court (1672-1679)
2) The Madonna della Salute, known as Mesopanditissa
3) The interior of the basilica
4) Cain and Abel, by Titian (1542-1544) (Sacristy)

5) David and Goliath, by Titian (1542-1544) (Sacristy)

Pages 34-35: The Marriage of Cana, by J. Robusti, better known as Tintoretto (1518-1594) (Sacristy) "Detail"

3

Basilica of the Frari

Founded towards the middle of the XIII century by the Franciscan Order of Minor Friars, then rebuilt to a design by an anonymous architect in its present Gothic style around 1330 and finished towards 1443, the Basilica of the Frari is the Venetian church most richly endowed with works of art after that of St. Mark. This is an example of rare simplicity and beauty with pure essential lines unspoiled by the ostentatious decoration common to much Gothic architecture. It is situated in the San Polo district overlooking Campo dei Frari, crossed by the Rio dei Frari, in an atmosphere of quiet and composed elegance. The reddish colour of the brick walls is in pleasant contrast with the Istrian stone used for the kiosks, the capitals and the other sober decorations of the doorways in the façade, the side entrances, and the beautiful Romanesque Bell Tower which is 70 metres high and the work of the Venetian architects Jacopo and Pier Paolo Celega. The façade, sober and elegant, in late Gothic style, is divided into three parts by pilasters surmounted by kiosks with capitals and columns in Veneto-Byzantine style. The lobed crowning outlines the upper edge with graceful curvature while the brick cornice, supported by small acute arches starts from

1) *The basilica seen from Rio dei Frari*
2) *Trinity Cloister*
3) *The apses of the basilica as seen from Campo S. Rocco*
4) *Lunette above the door of St. Mark's chapel*
5) *St. Ambrose door*

the façade and runs right along the sides of the church. On the great arched doorway, formed by slender, decorated columns in white Istrian stone are the statues of *Christ Risen* (by Alessandro Vittoria), *St. Francis* and the *Madonna* (by B. Bon). Three large rose windows open in correspondence with the nave and aisles on the inside. The Porta Mediana (the middle door), the Door of the Chapel of St. Peter, that of St. Ambrose, and that of St. Mark open on the left side of the Basilica. They too have decorative elements in Istrian stone. The solemn grace of the exterior complements the warm luminosity of the interior. The plan is that of a Latin cross divided into a nave and two aisles by twelve large pilasters which support ogival arches and which are interconnected by wooden beams. The *Friars' Choir* in the nave in front of the presby-

1) *Interior of the basilica*
2) *The internal facade with paintings by F. Floriani*
3) *Monument to Canova*
4) *Monument to the Doge Giovanni Pesaro*
5) *Holy water stoup by Girolamo Campagna*
6) *View of the right nave of the basilica*
7) *Lacunar from the San Francesco School and paintings by Vicentino*

tery was begun in Gothic form by the Bon workshop and finished in Renaissance style by the Lombardo family in 1475. A very fine cornice surmounts the classical arches of the central opening and supports a wooden Crucifixion and marble statues of the Apostles, the Virgin Mary, and St. John the Baptist. The work of the Cozzi family, wood carvers of Vicenza, the choir has 124 stalls and is a splendid example of the art of woodworking in Venice. Immediately on entering the church the eye is attracted to Titian's

sixteenth century work by Tullio Lombardo, and the monument to the Procurator of St. Marks Alvise Pasqualigo, presumably the work of Lorenzo Bregno. Over the doorway is the Baroque monument to Girolamo Garzoni who died in the siege of Negroponte in 1688. Along the left side aisle, the first altar is a 1663 work of Baldassare Longhena. Sculptures by Bernardo Falcone and Just Le Court, representing the various Virtues, decorate the altar while on the right hand wall the large canvas by Francesco

Assumption on the High Altar in all its splendid luminosity against the background of the window in the apse. Examining the Basilica from the internal façade, we shall move down the left aisle, the sacristy, the apse and the right aisle: a tour of the rich artistic patrimony of the Basilica. The internal façade whose richness is in contrast with the sobriety of the exterior, is decorated above by 8 canvasses by Flaminio Fiorani which represent the *Miracles of St. Anthony*, and one by Pietro Muttoni which represents St. Anthony of Padua and his Basilica. To the right and the left of the doorway respectively - the monument to Senator Pietro Bernardo, a

Rosa which belongs to the «dark» school, represents a Miracle of St. Anthony of Padua. Next is the monument to Titian, realized by pupils of Canova between 1838 and 1852 and judged as a cold and ponderous work. At the second altar the lovely canvas by Giuseppe Porta, called Salviati, represents the *Presentation of the Child Christ* at the Temple (1548), while at the third altar dedicated to St. Jospeh of Copertino and noteworthy as one of the finest works of the sixteenth century, is the statue of *St. Jeremy* sculpted by Alessandro Vittoria in 1565. It is considered his masterpiece. The painting *of St. Joseph of Copertino in Ecstacy* is the

1) The Assumption by Titian (1518): detail
2) The Assumption by Titian (1518)

work of Giuseppe Nogari. From the fourth altar, with the beautiful altarpiece by Palma the Younger of the *Martyrdom of St. Catherine* and the XVI, XVII and XVIII century funeral monuments, we move to the right arm of the transept. Of particular interest here is the tomb of *Jacopo Marcello*, which is claimed to be one of the most beautiful Venetian monuments. Simple and solemn, enclosed within an oval marble frame, it portrays the sea captain who died at Gallipoli in 1484, standing, clothed in armour, on the sarcophagus and attended by two pages. It is the work of Pietro Lombardo (XV cent.). We pass into the sacristy through the doorway framed by the elegant Renaissance monument to Benedetto Pesaro sea captain, with a fine statue of the deceased by Lorenzo Bregno. The sacristy, which was commissioned by the Pesaro family around the middle of the sixteenth century, has the proportions of a small church, and a rich collection of art treasures. Especially worthy of mention is the lovely *Madonna Enthroned with the Child and Saints*, a triptych by Giovanni Bellini, 1488, on the arch of the apse. This work, which is considered a masterpiece, is in a precious gilded frame carved by J. da Faenza. Leaving the sacristy, we see on the right the chapel of the Venetian family Bernardo, to which the beautiful Gothic tomb is dedicated. The work is attributed to De Santi or perhaps the Dalle Masegne family. The polyptych on the altar by Bartolomeo Vivarini,1482, is noteworthy for the happy use of colour and the strong stylization. It represents, in the centre the Madonna Enthroned and Child, on the left St. Andrew and St. Nicholas of Bari, on the right St. Paul and St. Peter, and above, the Dead Christ. The elegant Renaissance frame is attributed to Jacopo da Faenza. From the second apsidal chapel, or Chapel of the Holy Sacrament, with a fourteenth century monument to Arnaldo d'Este and the Gothic monument to the Florentine Ambassador Duccio Alberti, we move to the third, the Chapel of the Florentines, dominated by the beauty of the superb wooden statue of *John the Baptist*, 1438, Donatello's masterpiece. This is the only statue by Donatello

1) Triptych by Bellini
2) Triptych by Bellini: detail

1

2

which is still in Venice but one of great realism and expressive force. On reaching the presbytery one is struck by the architectural grandiosity and triumphant spirituality evoked by the filtered light from the large ogival windows. Titian's Assumption which makes a backcloth for the High Altar, is itself a source of light thanks to his extraordinary use of colour. This work, looked upon as the most precious in the Basilica, was completed in 1518 and became even more famous over the centuries to the point where Canova called it the most beautiful statue in the world, for the power and splendour with which Titian had imbued it, complemented by his exploitation of the very architecture of the Basilica itself. To the right and to the left of the presbytery we find the monument to Doge Francesco Foscari, the work of Antonio and Paolo Bregno in the transitional style between Gothic and Renaissance, and the *monument to Doge Nicolò Tron*, judged the most magnificent monument in Venice and a true Renaissance masterpiece, by Antonio Rizzo. Of the chapels in the left hand apse, *the first* is dedicated to the Franciscan Saints. The altarpiece is an admirable work by Bernardino Licino (1524) which represents the Madonna and Child between Saints Anthony, Ludovico of Tolosa, Francis, Bonaventura, Andrew and Mark. *In the second chapel*, of the Trevisan family, the monument to the military leader Melchiorre Trevisan is attributed to L. Bregno. *In the third chapel* that of the Milanese, is the particularly noteworthy and beautiful altarpiece depicting St. Ambrose enthroned between angel musicians and eight saints. The work was begun by Alvise Vivarini and finished in 1503 by Marco Basaiti. The fourth, the Corner Chapel or that of St. Mark, was added in about 1425 as part of the original design of the church. A fine statue of St. John the Baptist by Sansovino is above the baptismal font. A triptych of St. Mark enthroned between angel musicians and Sts. John the Baptist, Jerome, Nicholas and Paul, is a vigorous example of the art of B. Vivarini. Among the most beautiful

1) Equestrian monument to Paolo Savelli (Jacopo Della Quercia)
2) The Madonna di Ca' Pesaro by Titian (1519-1526)

examples of Venetian Renaissance style is the monument to Frederick Corner, of the Donatello school. The monochromatic fresco surrounding it is attributed to Andrea Mantegna. Another vibrant work by Titian in the left aisle is the *Madonna of Ca' Pesaro*, the Madonna and Child Enthroned and surrounded by various members of the Pesaro family. The Renaissance monument is dedicated to the Bishop of Cyprus and Venetian Commander against the Turks, Jacopo Pesaro. It is followed by the grandiose mausoleum of Doge Giovanni Pesaro, built around the side door of the Basilica, framing it. It was designed by Baldassare Longhena and built in polychrome marbles in a rich, but perhaps excessively insistent, Baroque style. And finally, in homage to Canova, the monument which he had originally designed for Titian's tomb (1794) was erected to him. Canova died before the work was completed and his pupils Bartolomeo Ferrari, Rinaldo Rinaldi, Luigi Zandomeneghi, Jacopo de' Martini and Antonio Bosa supervised the execution and had their master's heart sealed in a porphyry urn and placed in the monument. Extending to the right of the Basilica are the two vast cloisters of the ex-Convent of the Frari, called Ca' Grande, now the headquarters of the highly important State Archives which contain a rich and valuable documentation of the history of Venice.

1) Several stalls in the wooden choir located in the central nave
2) Paolo Veneziano: St. Francis and St. Elizabeth of Hungary (detail)

The Church of St. John and St. Paul

This church is situated in the square or Campo of the same name next to the marble façade of the Scuola Grande (Grand School) of St. Mark, now the Civic Hospital, and is an outstanding example of Gothic religious architecture. The building was begun in 1246, but only the lower part of the façade of the original construction is still in existence. It was finished and consacrated only in 1430 and became the favourite burial place for the doges and military leaders until today it is looked upon as the Pantheon of the Glories of the Venetian Republic. In sharp contrast to the white marble of the Renaissance School of St. Mark, the red brick of which this church is built, like the Basilica of the Frari, is decorated with quietly sober restraint. A cornice of small ogival arches starts from the façade and continues along the sides of the church and the bell tower, while a second double cornice in stone outlines the upper edge of the façade and is finished with three kiosks or tabernacles. A large rose window opens in the centre of the façade with a smaller one on either side to give light to the interior of the church. Round windows and two-lighted tall narrow mullions along the sides filter a warm light reflected from the brick walls, again like the Basilica of the Frari. In the lower part of the façade which as has been said dates back to the original construction, a series of blind arches enclose the tombs of Doges Jacopo and Lorenzo Tiepolo (1249 and 1275), Marco Michiel and Daniele Bon (1425). The great portal is a glorious example of the transitional style between Gothic and Renaissance, with two series of double columns at both sides supporting

1) *Aerial view of the basilica*
2) *Façade of the church, and to the right, the monument to Colleoni*
3) *Outside view of the Apse*
4) *The Sansovino well-curb*
5) *The tomb of the Doge Jacopo Tiepolo*
6-7) *St. Peter Martyr and St. Vincenzo Ferrer: bas-reliefs from the 15th century*

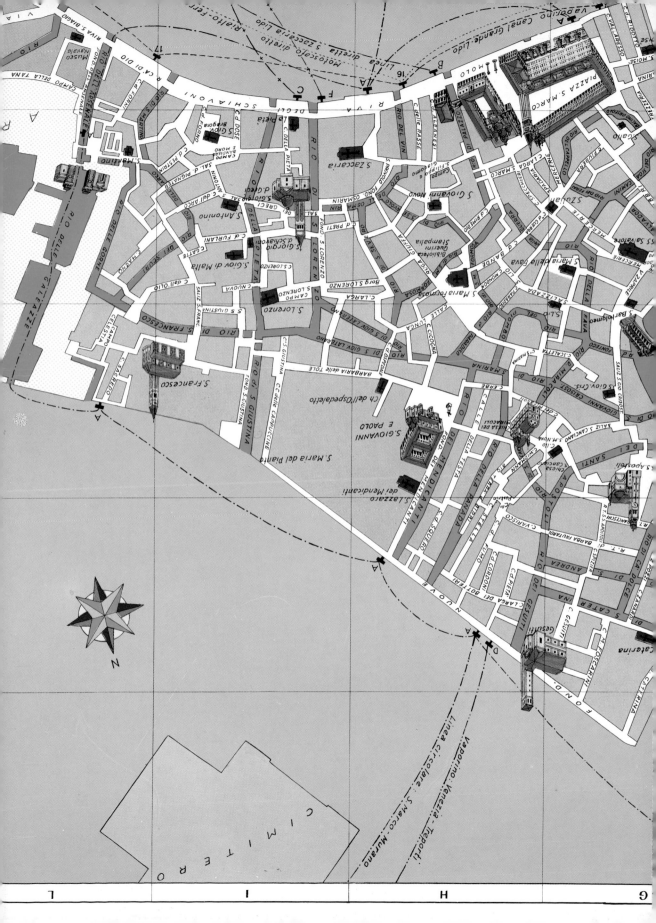

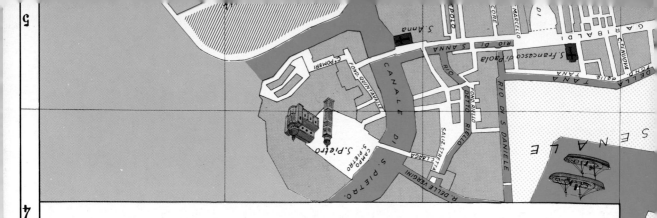

EDIFICI E MONUMENTI PIÙ IMPORTANTI * EDIFICES ET MONUMENTS LES PLUS IMPORTANTS * BUILDING AND MONUMENTS OF MOST INTEREST * DIE BEDEUTEND-STEN GEBÄUDE UND MONUMENTE * EDIFICIOS Y MONUMENTOS MÁS IMPORTANTES

(Un sistema di coordinate, con cifre e lettere permette di trovare nella pianta i punti desiderati)

Abbazia della Misericordia 1G	Chiesa S. Apostoli 3G	Palazzo Ducale 5H
Accademia Belle Arti 5E	Chiesa S. Giacomo di Rialto 3G	Palazzo Farsetti 4G
Arsenale 4L	Chiesa S. Francesco d. Vigna 3I	Palazzo Grassi 5E
Biblioteca Querini Stampalia 4H	Chiesa S. Giovanni e Paolo 3H	Palazzo Grimani 4F
Biennale d'Arte 6N	Chiesa S. Marco 4H	Palazzo Loredan 4G
Ca' d'Oro 3F	Chiesa S. Maria dei Gesuati 6E	Palazzo Mocenigo 4E
Ca' Foscari 5E	Chiesa S. Maria della Salute 6G	Palazzo Papadopoli 4F
Ca' Pesaro 3F	Chiesa S. Pietro di Castello 4N	Palazzo Pisani 4E
Ca' Rezzonico 5E	Chiesa S. Sebastiano 5D	Pescheria 3F
Ca' Vendramin Calergi 2F	Chiesa S. Zaccaria 4H	Piazza S. Marco 5G
Campanile di S. Marco 5H	Dogana 5G	Ponte Accademia 5E
Campo Manin 4G	Fontego dei Turchi 2E	Ponte Rialto 3G
Campo S. Bartolomeo 3G	Ghetto 1E	Ponte Scalzi 3D
Campo S. Luca 4G	Monumento Colleoni 3H	Ponte Sospiri 5H
Campo S. Polo 4F	Museo Navale 5L	Prigioni 5H
Campo S. Salvatore 4G	Ospedale Civile (Scuola S. Marco) 3H	San Giorgio (isola) 6I
Casa Tintoretto 1F	Palazzo Balbi 4E	Scala del Bovolo 4G
Chiesa Angelo Raffaele 5C	Palazzo Bernardo 4F	Scuola Carmini 5D
Chiesa Frari 4E	Palazzo Contarini 5E	Scuola S. Giorgio Schiavoni 4I
Chiesa Gesuiti 2G	Palazzo Corner 3F	Scuola S. Giovanni Ev. 3E
Chiesa Greci 4I	Palazzo Corner (Prefettura) 5F	Scuola S. Rocco 4E
Chiesa Madonna dell'Orto 1F	Palazzo Corner Spinelli 4F	Scuola S. Teodoro 4G
Chiesa Miracoli 3H	Palazzo Dario 6F	Teatro La Fenice 5F
Chiesa Redentore 7F		Teatro Verde 6I

LINEE DI NAVIGAZIONE LAGUNARE * LIGNES DE NAVIGATION LAGUNAIRE * LAGOON NAVIGATION LINES * SCHIFFAHRTSLINIEN IN DER LAGUNE * LINEAS DE NAVEGACION LAGUNAR

- Linea A - Circolare S. Marco-Murano.
- Linea B - Linea diretta S. Zaccaria-Lido.
- Linea C - Linea Venezia-Alberoni-S. Pietro in Volta-Pellestrina-Chioggia.
- Linea D - Linea Venezia-Murano-Burano-Torcello-Treporti.
- Linea E - Servizio trasporto automezzi Piazzale Roma-Lido-Punta Sabbioni.
- Linea F - Linea Venezia-Punta Sabbioni.
- Servizio vaporino Piazzale Roma-Lido (approdi dal n. 1 al n. 19).
- Servizio motoscafi Piazzale Roma-Rio Nuovo-Lido (approdi senza numero).
- Servizio motoscafi da Rialto-Piazzale Roma (Canal Grande).

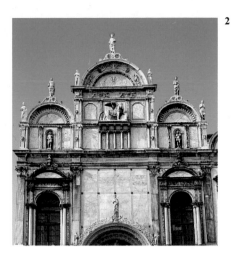

a great ogival archway. The work was begun by B. Bon as part of a project which was never completed for the rebuilding of the whole façade. The interior of the Church, with the wide ogival archway and cross vaulting strikes one immediately for the harmony yet also power of its spaciousness and for the evocative lighting. The ogival arches and the walls are connected, as in the Basilica of the Frari, by a system of wooden tie-beams which intersect the upper space with not ungraceful lines. Their function is to substitute the flying buttresses and counterforts in other Gothic churches. The Church is built in the form of a Greek cross with the interior divided into a nave and two side aisles by ten cylindrical pilasters. We shall tour the Church, starting from the internal façade and proceeding along the nave, the right transept, the presbytery, the left transept and the left aisle. The whole internal wall of the façade is occupied by one monument in Lombard style to Bartolomeo Bragadin (+ 1507) and three monuments to the Mocenigo family: the tomb of Doge Alvise (1577) and his wife, a rather classical work by Grapiglia; the tomb of Giovanni Mocenigo by Tullio Lombardo and that which is considered Pietro Lombardo's masterpiece - the *monument to Doge Pietro Mocenigo*, with three virile figures supporting the sarcophagus, framed by an arch with six statues of young warriors in niches at the sides. The statue of the Doge clothed in armour and flanked by two pages stands on top of the sarcophagus. In order along the right aisle are the tomb of Doge Ranieri Zeno; the first altar with a painting by F. Bissolo of the Bellini school, an

2 Enthroned Madonna and Child with Eight Saints; the monument to the heroic defender of Famagosta who was flayed alive by the Turks in 1571, Antonio Bragadin. His skin is preserved in the urn on the monument, a sign of the Venetians' homage to the martyr of Venice. At the second altar: the beautiful early work by G. Bellini, the *polyptych of St. Vincenzo Ferreri* is a masterpiece of the early Renaissance in Venice. There are signs of the influence of Mantegna's painting combined with that sense of colour which was to become typical of Bellini's later works. In the centre of the polyptych, St. Vincenzo Ferreri is between St. Christopher and St. Sebastian; at the top the Dead Christ; the Archangel Gabriel, and the Annunciation; in the three panels of the predella, episodes from the life of St. Vincenzo Ferreri. The next monument is that of Alvise Valier, Senator of the Republic (+ 1589); the Gothic Chapel of Our Lady of Sorrows with later Baroque decoration; the sumptuously Baroque Valier mausoleum by A. Tirali (1708); the Chapel of Peace with a Madonna and Child, a Byzantine work of the XII-XIII century; the grandiose Chapel of St. Dominic at the end of the aisle with a splendid canvas painted by G.B. Piazzetti in 1727 of the Glory of St. Dominic. This work is considered a masterpiece of eighteenth century Venetian painting. Arriving at the transept, among the monuments and paintings of particular interest are Alvise Vivarini's *Christ Carrying the Cross*, 1474; and the lovely altarpiece by Lorenzo Lotto of *The Alms of St. Antonino*, dated 1542. Then follows the monument to Dionigi Aldo of Brisighella, a General of the Serenissima, with statues by L. Bregno and, above, a *large magnificent window* with Gothic tracery filled with beautiful stained glass painted by G. A. Licinio of Lodi to cartoons by Vivarini, Cima, and Mocatto. The two apsidal chapels, the Chapel of the Crucifixion and the Chapel of the *Magdalen* contain, the first, bronze statues by Vittoria; the second an elegant marble triptych by Bergamasco of Magdalen between St.

1) Monument to Bartolomeo Colleoni, a work by Verrocchio
2) The Grande Scuola of St. Mark, end section

Andrew and St. Philip. The apse of the presbytery is lit by five orders of two-light windows which illuminate the fine High Altar attributed to Longhena. The monuments on the surrounding walls are, on the right, to Doge Michele Morosini and Doge Leonardo Loredan; that on the left which is considered a Venetian masterpiece of the Venetian funeral art of the fifteenth century - the monument to Doge Andrea Vendramin. Some historians attribute the architectural part of this work to Pietro Lombardo (it seems that the Lombardo family did in fact have a contract for the doges' monuments in the XV century), others to Leopardi. The very fine bas-reliefs are certainly the work of Antonio Lombardo and the classical style statues, of Tullio Lombardo. Turning to the left, we find the apsidal Chapel of the Holy Trinity and the Cavalli or St. Pius V Chapel which contain respectively, the tombs of Pietro Corner and Andrea Morosini; and Jacopo and Marino Cavalli besides the urn of Doge Giovanni Dolfin. From the left transept one enters the Chapel of the Rosary. Restored in 1913 and reacquiring its original appearance after it had been practically destroyed by fire in 1867, the chapel preserves what remains of a

1) View of central apse and right cross, with large Gothic window
2) Interior of the church
3) View of the Chapel of the Blessed Giacomo Salomoni
4) Monument to the Doge Pietro Mocenigo by Pietro Lombardo
5) St. Jerome by A. Vittoria
6) Vendramini Monument: detail - St. Catherine

1

rich artistic patrimony of sculptures by Vittoria and G. Campagna, and paintings by Tintoretto, Palma the Younger, Bassano and others. There are three works by Veronese set into the Lorenzetti ceiling. It is still possible to admire two splendid *reredos* in wood carved by G. Piazzetta in 1698. Particularly noteworthy among the numerous important works of art is the lovely painting of the *Archangel Michael Striking Lucifer*, of uncertain attribution. The left aisle also contains numerous funeral monuments to doges and military leaders of the Venetian Republic. Among these we mention the monument to Doge Pasquale Malpiero (+1462) in Renaissance style, the first of its kind in Venice, by Pietro Lombardo. Another monument of particular interest is that to *Doge Tommaso Mocenigo* (+ 1423): this is the work of the Tuscan master artistis Pietro Lamberti and G. di Martino of Fiesole, with sculptures showing the influence of Donatello. A marble canopy held up by two *angels* shelters the sarcophagus on which is a *statue* of the Doge. A statue of Justice surmounts the canopy while a splendid Gothic style reredos acts as background to the monument. The *monument to Doge Nicolo Marcello*, by Pietro Lombardo, is in pure Renaissance style, as is the altar by Bergamasco which it dominates. The lovely statue of *St. Jerome* is the work of Vittoria. Outside the Church, continuing the theme of the numerous monuments to Venetian military leaders on the inside, we find the equestrian monument to Bartolomeo Colleoni, who led the army of the republic during its expansion on the mainland in the fifteenth century. Designed by Verrocchio, the statue was executed by A. Leopardi.

1) *Mausoleum of the Doges Bertucci and Silvestro Valier*
2) *Monument to Senator G. Bonzio*
3) *Monument to the Doge Pasquale Malipiero by P. Lombardo*
4) *Polyptych by G. Bellini*

Museum and Palaces

Along the sides of the Grand Canal which crosses the city in great wide curves, are the most beautiful Venetian palaces, architectural treasures in themselves, and in some cases the treasure houses of the most important art collections. Thus, that which for Venice is the central means of communication, is also to a certain extent the centre of its cultural life and the most spectacular route for the visiting tourist. *The Ca' d'Oro* (House of Gold), the most famous palace on the Grand Canal, commissioned by Marino Contarini in the first half of the fifteenth century, is an illustrious example of the decorated Gothic style which was gradually developing in Venice at that time. While six single-light windows open on the right side of the façade, the left side is a mass of intricate embroidery with a portico on the ground floor and two loggias on the upper floors with interwoven arches in an elegant and complex design. After the various restorations and alterations nothing remains of the gilding of the ornamental parts of the façade which gave the palace its name. Left to the State by its last owner, Baron Franchetti, it now houses the Franchetti Gallery which has a rich collection of art works of the Veneto school including a St. Sebastian by Mantegna and a *Polyptych* by A. Vivarini. *Palazzo Pesaro*, on the other hand, is an example of seventeenth century architecture. Begun by Longhena in 1660 and finished by Antonio Gaspari, it is certainly the most sumptuous palace of the Baroque period. In addition to the Oriental Museum, since 1897 it has housed the International Gallery of Modern Art which, with the Biennial Exhibition of Art held every two years, offers a regular cultural appointment among the most important and discussed in Italy. The gallery's collection covers nineteenth and twentieth century Venetian painting and also numerous and noteworty examples of Italian painting: from Hayez to Fattori, Signorini, De Chirico, Campigli, Casorati, Boccioni, Rosai, Morlotti, Vedova and Birolli. And with the Italians also various examples of the European avant-garde: from Matisse to Chagall, Max Ernst, Tobey, Klee and Kandinsky. *The Palazzo Ducale*. The Ducal Palace or Doge's Palace, which we shall discuss more fully later has, like the Ca' d'Oro, elegant decorated Gothic embellishments and in its rooms a rich patrimony of paintings of the Veneto school, a true and proper art gallery with important works by Veronese, Tintoretto and Titian. The ideal continuation of the Ducal Palace collection is that of the *Ca' Rezzonico*, home of the Museum of Venetian paintings of the eighteenth century, a time of great developments in Venetian art. From painting to the applied arts Ca' Rezzonico, an elegant residence of Sansovinian inspiration, represents a rich testimony to the taste and the way of life of the Venetian aristocracy in the XVIII century. The artistic patrimony of the *Gallerie dell'Accademia* (the Academy Gallery), which we shall mention again later is, on the other hand, particularly well endowed with works of the fifteenth century while also having a significant collection from other periods. Then, overlooking the Grand Canal we have *Palazzo Gritti*, another example of the Gothic style with a fine brick façade, and *Palazzo Vendramin Calergi*, originally belonging to the Loredan family and considered a masterpiece of the Venetian Renaissance. Finished towards 1500 by Codussi, the Vendramin Calergi Palace was then decorated by Giorgione and perhaps by Titian, but nothing remains of those frescoes today. If wishing to continue the tour along the Grand Canal it is well worth while visiting *Palazzo Corner* by Sansovino and *Palazzo Grimani* by Sanmicheli, both XVI century palaces; and the most important eighteenth century palace, Palazzo Grassi, the work of Massari. But the tour of the museums must not miss out the Scuola Grande di San Rocco (the Grand School of San Rocco), a little away from the Grand Canal on the Rio della Frescada, with an excellent collection of works by Tintoretto.

The Ducal Palace

The Ducal Palace, or Palace of the Doges, is the largest and most splendid civic building in Venice, theatre of all the political history of the Republic. It overlooks the Piazzetta (the square) and the quay at St. Mark's Basin offering to visitors arriving by sea, a lovely view of the chromatic harmony of its façades and the elegant grace of its arches in a scene of rare beauty and stylistic composition which includes St. Mark's Basin, with the Clock Tower and the Bell Tower. It was the seat of the doges and the high magistrature of the Republic at one time and then passed to the use of government offices and cultural organizations. It was built in place of the old embattled castle which had been erected in the year 814 and was destroyed by fire in 976 and again in 1105. The present architectural appearance began to take shape in the first half of 1300 when the structure of the old castle was considered to be too out of date, and passed through three distinct phases of construction supervised by

1) View of the Ducal Palace, seat of the Doge and the highest courts of the Republic
2) Capital with winged lion
3) Capital with statue of the first patron of Venice: St. Theodore
4) View of Ducal Palace
5-6) Two openings for making secret accusations

DENONTIE SECRETE
CONTRO CHI OCCVLTERÃ
GRATIE ET OFFICII.
Õ COLLVDERÃ PER
NASCONDER LA VERA
RENDITA D̃ ESSI

DENONTIE SECRETE CONTRO
CONTRABANDIERI.
ET TRASGRESSORLO
IN OGNI SORTE DI OGLI

architects and artists such as the Dalle Masegne family, Pietro Lamberti, A. Rizzo, P. Lombardo, S. Spavento, the Scarpagnino and several others. The Hall of the Great Council which overlooks St. Mark's Basin, and the part overlooking the Piazzetta as far as the sixth arch, were built during the first phase. The wing along the Rio del Palazzo, whose inner façade was rebuilt by A. Rizzo at a later date, was added in a second phase. The third stage continued the side facing the Piazzetta as far as St. Mark's Basilica after demolition of the building which still stood between the Palace and the Church. With the interior decorated by numerous paintings of the Veneto school, a true and proper art gallery, the Doge's Palace remained practically unchanged in appearance for about four centuries in spite of the fact that it was damaged by fire numbers of times in addition to those already mentioned in the remote past. The two main façades, exactly matching, which look over the Piazzetta and St. Mark's Basin, are in three orders: on ground level an arcade with wide pointed arches; above that an open loggia with quatrefoil arches, two for each one below; above the loggia is a smooth wall with ogival windows and small round windows above those, the whole wall surface being decorated by a geometrical design of white, grey and red marble lozenges with a particularly successful chromatic effect. The Veneto-Byzantine crenellations outlining the top of the wall recall the white embroidery of the vault and the portico of the gallery below. From the *Porta della Carta* (Gate of the Papers), the splendidly majestic entrance, the work of G. and B. Bon, the visitor enters the courtyard of the Palace: with majestic dimensions and strangely evocative atmosphere, the courtyard is enclosed by the internal façades of the Palace, elegant and richly decorated with Gothic, Renaissance and almost classical motives, the work of such artists as A. Rizzo, the Lombards, the Scarpagnino and Monopola. On the north side of the Courtyard, against the background of the dome of St. Mark's, one finds the Foscari Portico and the Foscari *Arch*, a Venetian Gothic style construction with Renaissance elements. And standing in front of the Foscari Arch, the *Giant's Staircase* by Antonio Rizzo, with two gigantic statues of *Neptune* and *Mars*, both the work of Sansovino. The *Clock*

Façade, an unusual work by Monopola can be seen above the Foscari Portico. The *Censors' Staircase* leads from the ground floor to the loggias which open towards the courtyard on three sides and on the exterior on two façades. Here one faces the beautiful *Foscari Loggia which* was opened towards the Piazzetta under the dogate of Francesco Foscari. To reach the two upper floors, one ascends the *Golden Staircase*, a beautiful sixteenth century work executed by Scarpagnino to a design by Sansovini, and originally used only by the magistrates and other personalities. Among the numerous rooms on the *first piano nobile* or noble floor as it is called, are those of the members of the high magistrature, the *Hall of the Great Council*, the *Hall of the Scrutiny*, the *Hall of the Criminal Magistrate* and the *Hall of the Civil Law Magistrate*, and also that which at one time was the Doge's lodging. All the rooms, and there are many others we have not mentioned, still contain in their original position on the walls and ceilings innumerable works of art of inestimable value, in equally precious frames which add the richness of their design to the beauty of the paintings. In the Great Council Hall, for example, lit by reflections from St.

1) *Courtyard of the Ducal Palace*
2) *Detail of the sixteenth century façade with two levels of loggias*
3) *The Giants' Staircase*

3

Mark's Basin, there is a large painting of *Paradise* by the Tintorettos, father and son; and the *Apotheosis of Venice* by Paolo Veronese. A number of other works by these artists were destroyed in the fire of 1577, along with others by Vivarini, Pisanello, Carpaccio, Titian. In the Hall of the Scrutiny, a work of special importance is the *Last Judgement* by Palma the Younger. The famous statues of *Adam* and *Eve*, sculpted by Antonio Rizzo are in the Hall of the Civil Law Magistrate. A narrow corridor leads from this hall, over the *Bridge of Sighs* to the New Prisons. Among works by Carpaccio, Bellini and

others in the Doge's lodgings, there are some interesting paintings by Jeronimus Bosch, the so-called «stregozzi» of satirical inspiration. From this 'piano nobile' a staircase leads to the Doge's private chapel where one finds a fine fresco painted by Titian, of *St. Christopher*, at the request of Doge Andrea Gritti

The Great Council hall: this is the largest hall in the palace, where about one thousand electors of the Doge and other high offices gathered

during 1523 to 1524. Continuing up the Golden Staircase one reaches the second noble floor, divided, like the other, into numerous rooms for use as government offices, and also richly endowed with works of art. An extraordinary and very valuable collection of weapons of war is kept in the Armoury of the Council of Ten. Firearms and cutting weapons, they go back to the XV and XVI centuries. The works of art include in particular Doge Grimani Kneeling before Faith, by Titian, which is in the Hall of the Four Doors; *Mercury and the Graces* and *Bacchus and Ariadne by Jacopo Tintoretto* and the *Rape of Europa* by Paolo Veronese, all in the Antecollege; *Venice Enthroned* by Veronese on the ceiling of the magnificent Hall of the College and, on a wall of the same Hall, various fine works by Tintoretto, including the *Marriage of St. Catherine*. There are numerous other valuable works which we do not mention here but which adorn the rooms of the Palace with themes which record in a pictorial narrative, moments in the history of the Serenissima. That same history which has always celebrated its most important moments in the Ducal Palace, the very heart of Civic Power.

The Golden Staircase: sumptuous staircase ornamented with stucco work by Vittoria and frescoes by Franco connects the principal loggia with the Collegio and Santo Hall. To the right, the Bridge of Sighs

Academy of Fine Arts

The Academy Gallery is of considerable importance for the rich patrimony of Venetian paintings it contains and which are exhibited in historical order from the fourteenth to the eighteenth century. The «Academy of Sculptors and Painters» as it was called originally, was founded in 1750 under the direction of Piazzetta and a few years later passed under the direction of Tiepolo. In 1807 Napoleon Bonaparte instituted the Academy of Fine Arts which was then moved to the present building with the first nucleus of eighteenth century works which had been collected up to that time. The collection gradually grew as a result of private donations and also after the transfer to the Academy of the artistic patrimonies of the religious bodies which had been suppressed by Napoleon, and also thanks to acquisitions on the part of the State and restitutions on the part of Austria after the Treaty of St. Germain in 1919. For the fourteenth century we should mention the great polyptych by Lorenzo Veneziano of *The Annunciation, Saints and Prophets* in the first room of the Gallery, and *St. Lawrence* and the *Madonna Enthroned and Child and Pius Persons* by Nicolò di Pietro, besides numerous interesting works by lesser artists of the Venetian school. For the fifteenth century, notable works include *The Legend of St. Ursula*, a series of splendid canvasses by Carpaccio executed between 1490 and 1496 depicting the legend of the princess of Brittany who was killed with 11000 other virgins of her country by the Huns, during her pilgrimage to all the sanctuaries in the world. Still from the fifteenth century, the *Sacred Conversation* or Altarpiece of St. Job, by G. Bellini (1485), noteworthy for the delicate chromatic unity and formal severity and the *St. George* by Mantegna, a small, precious tablet of

1) Entry to the Galleries of the Accademia next to the Scuola della Carità
2) Cima da Conegliano: lament to the death of Christ (detail)
3) Tintoretto: portrait of Jacopo Soranzo 3 →

IACOBVS SVPERANTIO MDXVII

rare compositive perfection. For the sixteenth century, the best known work is perhaps *The Tempest* by Giorgione (1505-07), where the use of colour is truly splendid and the importance of the landscape which, from a simple background becomes a subject of creative inspiration, is without precedent. Another work of the sixteenth century is Titian's *St. John the Baptist* and the *Pietà*: this is an example of the latest development of Titian's art and interesting for its luminosity. Intended for the Church of the Frari, it was finished after the death of the master, by Palma the Younger. Other noteworthy works include The *Miracle of St. Mark* by Tintoretto, of great dramatic force and the famous masterpiece of Paolo Veronese *The Feast in the House of Levi* which, considered scandalous in some respects, caused the artist to be tried by the Inquisition. The seventeenth century is represented by works by Strozzi, Maffei, Mazzoni and others, while the eighteenth century includes works by Canaletto, the Longhi family, Guardi and also Tiepolo, Piazzetta and Rosalba Carriera.

Andrea Mantegna: St. George (detail). To the right the legend of St. Ursula: Carpaccio (detail)

1) *Carpaccio: Arrival of Pilgrims in Cologne (detail)*
2) *Giorgione: The Tempest (detail)*

Ca' Rezzonico

Headquarters of the museum of eighteenth century Venetian painting, Ca' Rezzonico with its elegant balconies divided by Doric semicolumns, of Sansovino influence, faces towards the Grand Canal. In the interior, a fine ceremonial staircase, the work of Giorgio Massari, adorned by two sculptures by J. Lecourt *Autumn* and *Winter*, leads to the upper floors. In the second half of the seventeenth century Filippo Bon, a Venetian nobleman, commissioned Baldassare Longhena to build the palace but it was completed only in 1745 by Giorgio Massari, when ownership of the palace passed to the Rezzonico family. Venice was at the height of its creative revival in all the arts: music, theatre, painting. A happy, lively spirit ran through the various expressions of this revival; one need only think of Boccherini and Vivaldi for music, Goldoni for the theatre, and the sparkling rococo of Sebastiano Ricci. But among all the arts, it was painting which demonstrated the greatest revival, both in the development of new kinds of painting, and for the extraordinary novelty of the expressive language and the large numbers of outstanding artists. The extraordinary personality of *Gian Battista Tiepolo* dominated them all. He was in demand at all the courts of Europe, known for his original use of colour, impetuous and striking, and for the dramatic effect of his compositions. *Pietro Longhi* painted in a satirical vein the customs of contemporary society; that same society that *Rosalba Carriera* was to portray in delightful, lively portraits in pastels. *Luca Carlevarijs*, *Antonio Canal, called Canaletto*, and *Francesco Guardi* began to paint views giving special attention to perspective, and so began the fashion for landscape painting which was soon to become popular all over Europe and was further developed in France and England in the following century. Ca' Rezzonico has a rich collection of specimens of Venetian painting of this happy period, which represent a completion of the collection preserved in the Academy. However, the museum's collection is not limited to eighteenth century paintings: it has also numerous examples of furniture, ceramics, Murano glassware, lacquered objects, cloth and Chinese objects in addition to a collection of costumes, all of which indicate the taste and way of life of the Venetian aristocracy and, with the pictorial patrimony; mirror the culture of the eighteenth century.

1) View of Ca' Rezzonico from the Grand Canal
2) Hanging lamp in the Brustolon hall

The School of San Rocco

Situated on the Campo di San Rocco, next to the Church of San Rocco, the School was built by Antonio Scarpagnino in 1549 to a design by Bartolomeo Bon, who had begun the construction in 1515 for the Brotherhood of San Rocco. In 1564 a competition was announced for the internal decoration and the most noted artists in Venice participated: Veronese, Schiavone, Salviati, Tintoretto, Zuccheri. It was won by Tintoretto who entered his *San Rocco in Gloria*, which is now in the ceiling of the lodging, and thus was entrusted with the work which he carried out between the years 1564 and 1588. The beautiful façade of the School on which one can clearly see the work done at various times by Bon and by Scarpagnino, owes the ground floor with its elegant two-light windows interspaced with Corinthian columns, to the former, and the upper floor on which the motive of the Corinthian columns which separate the double windows is repeated below a single entablature, to the latter. The main doorway is also Scarpagnino's work. One enters the interior however, via the doorway on the left side, directly into a large hall. The three phases in which the decoration of the School was carried out, begin chronologically from the paintings in the so-called hall of the lodging on the upper floor. Consequently it would be preferable to examine Tintoretto's works starting from this room, next to the Great Hall, which is reached by ascending the *great stairway* designed by Scarpagnino and decorated, on the walls, by the famous painting by A. Zanchi *The Plague in 1630* and that by Pietro Negri on the same theme. *The San Rocco in Gloria* is between the gilded carvings on the ceiling in the Hall of the Lodging. On the entrance wall, *Christ before Pilate*, Ecce Homo and the Way to Calvary and on the wall in front, the immense painting of *The*

The Upper Hall with its rich ceiling, decorated with twenty-one paintings by Tintoretto depicting scenes from the Old Testament.

Crucifixion, dramatic and inspiring. In an atmosphere of gloom and sadness, the ferocious determination of the squires and the indifference of the soldiers attending the sentence are in great contrast with the pain of the group in the foreground, with the Mother in the middle. The Upper Hall contains the numerous decorations done by Tintoretto in the second phase of the work: twenty-one canvasses cover the ceiling with subjects from the Old Testament; on the walls, twelve stories from the Old and New Testament: the *Last Supper*, the *Sernom in the Orchard*, the Nativity, the Baptism, the Resurrection, and again *St. Sebastian* and *St. Rocco*, *Christ Tempted*, the *Pool of Bethesda*, the *Ascension*, the *Resurrection of Lazzarus*, the *Multiplication of the Loaves and Fishes*. Some fine works by other masters are found side by side with those of Tintoretto, as, for example, Titian's Annunciation, 1525, and two beautiful early works by Gian Battista Tiepolo: *Abraham and the Angels* and *Agar Abandoned*. The altar in the Hall is the work of Bernardino (1528) while Giovanni Marchiori (1741) did the splendid carving on wood in the presbytery depicting the *Stories of San Rocco*, which is considered a true masterpiece of Venetian sculpture of the XVII century. Francesco Pianta the Younger carved the twelve caryatids in wood on the wall in front of the entrance, and, among these, a caricature of Tintoretto. A visit must be made to the rich patrimony of artistic objects which

*1) The Annunciation (detail). This commences
the series of large paintings dedicated to the
Virgin which are located in the majestic hall
on the ground floor.*

*2) The Slaughter of the Innocents (detail).
This is one of Tintoretto's most dramatic
works.*

represent the Treasure: sacred vessels belonging to the School, the School's statutes in ancient bindings, ancient gold objects of the Church.

The majestic Hall on the ground floor is divided into a nave and two aisles by two rows of Corinthian columns and is decorated with Tintoretto's last eight works, placed between the double windows: the *Annunciation*, with vivid chiaroscuro contrasts, the *Epiphany* or *Adoration of the Magi*, an interesting scenic composition, the *Flight into Egypt*, a real masterpiece of the artist's maturity, the *Slaughter of the Innocents*, two evocative night pictures of *St. Mary Magdalen* and *St. Mary the Egyptian*, the *Circumcision* and the *Assumption* which portrays the Virgin in an attitude of benediction rising towards the heavens in an explosion of light.

The crucifixion. Completed in 1565, it dominates the back wall of the Albergo Hall and is the largest and most spectacular painting from the Scuola of San Rocco.

Corror Museum

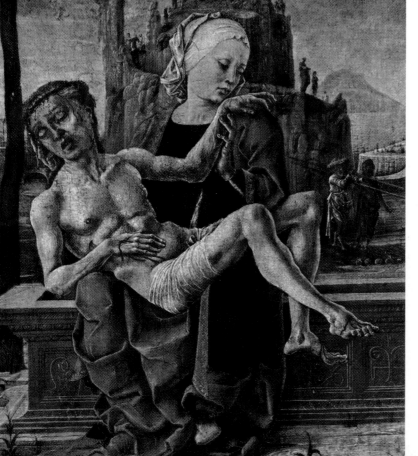

1) Gentile Bellini
The Doge Giovanni Mecenigo
Gentile, the brother of Giovanni Bellini, was called to the Orient in 1479 by the Sultan Mohammed II. Quite probably the portrait of the Doge, which he had been given a special appointment to paint, was left unfinished upon his departure. This is one of the finest portraits by the artist, and is as incisive as one of his famous medallions.

2) C. Tura. Pietà (part.)
One of the extremely rare works by the leader of the Ferrarese school, done around 1465. Tura based it on the monumental vision of Donatello that he acquired in Padua, and includes hints of Flemish verism, which could certainly be seen at the Ferrarese court. In fact, the expressionistic deformations of his figures probably come from the style of Van der Weyden.

3) V. Carpaccio
Man With a Red Cap
One of the most mysterious and evocative portraits of the last decade of the 15th century in Venice. The portrait was probably done by Carpaccio, especially if one accepts the theory that he was trained in Ferrara. The air of great pride, the incisiveness of the details, and the excellent color make it a true masterpiece, to be placed near the gentlemen gathered in the famous paintings of the ambassadors in the St. Ursula series, now hanging in the galleries of the Accademia (circa 1500).

3

The School of San Giorgio degli Schiavoni

1) V. Carpaccio
St. Augustine in His Study
This is the first painting of the legend of St. Jerome, done around 1502. St. Augustine, a musicologist and translator of the Scriptures, hears a divine voice telling him that St. Jerome is dead, and decides to go to see his mortal remains.
Carpaccio depicts the interior of the Saint's study as a symbolic setting, almost idealized but still intimately real, where the modern humanist addresses the problems of knowledge and history.
Even the face of the Saint is symbolic, and probably recalls the features of the famous Hellenist Bessarione, who donated his precious codices to the Libreria Marciana.

2) V. Carpaccio
The Funeral of St. Jerome. The funeral of St. Jerome is depicted on bare rock in the convent arcade.
The painter wanted to depict a scene in a mythical Orient where the palm trees and lions give a touch of credibility.
He is extraordinarily attentive to and even shows a touch of subtle humor in his depiction of the monks and clergymen attending the ceremony, who are dressed in cloaks in a bright blue that seems to shimmer in the sun.

3) V. Carpaccio
Baptism of the Emperor: Triumph of St. George (part.)
These are two scenes from the legend of St. George, the patron of chivalry, as told by Carpaccio for the school of San Giorgio degli Schiavoni between 1502 and 1507. The adventures of the Saint, which take place in a fabulous Orient, give the painter the opportunity to add real-life figures and costumes taken from Venice as well as a probable trip to those far-off countries. Carpaccio depicts a magical world in which reality, investigated through his meticulous and precise drawing, comes to life in a riot of colors.

The City

It is possible that no city in the world is as much photographed as Venice, and it is equally possible that no city in the world lends itself to so many different and contrasting interpretations as does Venice. Venice, the monumental city; Venice the city-museum; Venice sinking; Venice raised up and sparkling; Venice abandoned and left to die; Venice of the Venetians and the Venice of mass tourism, superficial and wasteful. These are all the many faces of Venice which in their inherent contradictions support the multiform and extraordinary character of the city, both in the variety of the sentiments which, from time to time, are invoked in the visitor, and in the complexity and dialectics of the endless debate on the historical problem of the destiny of the lagoon city. It is well known that the survival of Venice as an urban entity is threatened. And it is, also from a physical point of view, due to the progressive sinking of the city with respect to the level of the water; and from a social point of view because of its basic productive structure and environmental problems which cause a growing number of Venetians to move to the mainland. It is undeniable that in the evening, except during the so-called season, Venice is empty, silent, and melancholy, just as in the day it is full of life and activity. The romantic and decadent myth of the lagoon city has its roots in these aspects of nostalgic, extenuated beauty which dates from the end of the political vitality of the city, at the end of the last century when Venice, having lost its freedom, lost also its sense of dominion over its own historic destiny. The development of tourism and the various activities connected with it have, on the one hand, revived the economic situation of the city, but on the other, risk causing the end of its suburban vocation and turning Venice into a drawing-room or a museum, a silent ghost, rich only in its own beauty. Venice naturally invites such reflections because its charm is such, and such is the magic of its daily life, so rare and special its sense of the colour, the spaciousness and the tempo it transmits, that it is impossible not to consider the question of the future of this urban jewel. In Venice everything is mixed up together: monuments, churches, palaces, and houses of the common people, and all live side by side harmoniously interwoven without strident disaccord. It is as if the refinement of the architecture, the splendour of the decorations, and the beauty were in fact being offered to the eyes of the beholder quite unofficially, without pomp, as a natural gift from the city to the person who passes through it. Children play ball and ride bicycles between fine buildings in the campi and squares safe from urban traffic, which can offer no unexpected danger here any more than in an enclosed courtyard. Their cries and the sound of passers by, the noise of a large boat on the nearby canal, all combine to make the music of Venice. In Venice, as everyone knows, urban traffic is either on foot or by water so the city is free of all the noises of brakes, tyres, horns and railways which in other cities constitute the sound track of a sad daily documentary where the sound of footsteps is little more than a memory. It may be because Venice has another kind of music, where human beings are more noticeable and present, that it also has a different spirit and invites one to enjoy its beauties easily and naturally. Here the coming and going of steamboats marks the highway of a quiet acquatic metropolis. From the railway station to Piazza San Marco along the Grand Canal, the water imposes a slow rhythm. Speed is not permitted and since the availability of time is a good incentive to contemplation, it can happen that even a distracted tourist or a Venetian accustomed to Venice finds himself overwhelmed by the joy of his eyes.

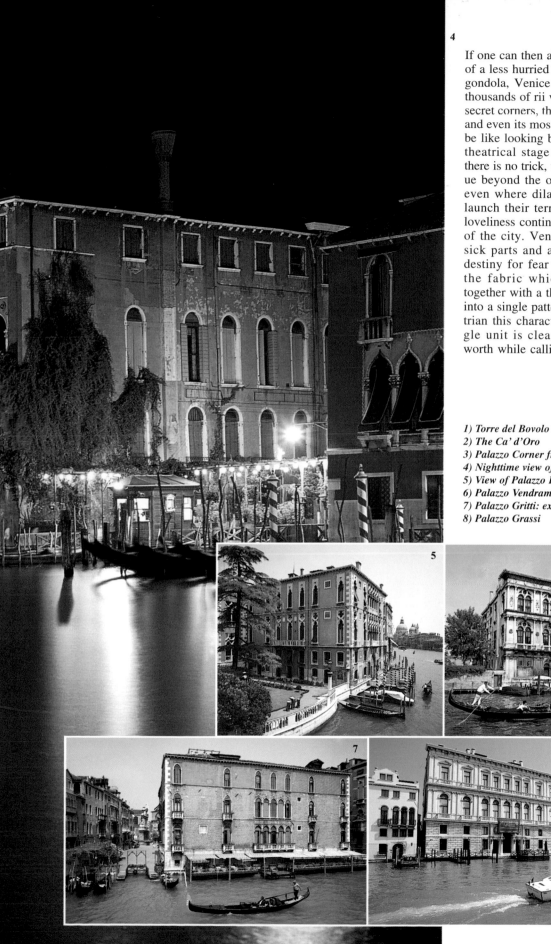

4

If one can then allow oneself the luxury of a less hurried tour, even perhaps in a gondola, Venice can reveal, among the thousands of rii which cross it, the most secret corners, the less obvious beauties, and even its most hidden injuries. It will be like looking behind the curtains of a theatrical stage only to discover that there is no trick, that the beauties continue beyond the official appearance and even where dilapidation and abandon launch their terrible warning, still the loveliness continues throughout the rest of the city. Venice cannot cut out the sick parts and abandon them to their destiny for fear of slowly unravelling the fabric which holds everything together with a thousand threads woven into a single pattern. Even to the pedestrian this characteristic of being a single unit is clear to see. It would be worth while calling at some of the inns

1) *Torre del Bovolo*
2) *The Ca' d'Oro*
3) *Palazzo Corner from Ca' Grande*
4) *Nighttime view of the Ca' d'Oro*
5) *View of Palazzo Franchetti*
6) *Palazzo Vendramin Calergi*
7) *Palazzo Gritti: example of Gothic style*
8) *Palazzo Grassi*

where it is still possible to sample Venetian delicacies based on fish with a glass of good wine. Or one can visit the «squeri» and see gondolas being built, or stop at the shop of a restorer or craftsman in glass work, or even allow oneself a moment of society life taking coffee at the tables of a bar in Piazza San Marco when one comes out unexpectedly in front of the splendour of the Basilica from the labyrinth of narrow calli (streets) nearby. From narrow streets between the walls of houses so close as to touch each other, with the odd line of washing hung out at the top to dry, one passes through squares of various sizes and into sudden light, spacious openings of wide perspective. Then immediately one is swallowed up again in a long sinuous calle, up and down bridges, between sudden reappearances of water and by the impression of being on terrafirma. It would be helpful for the visitor on his first visit, if he were to get an idea of the topography of the city and the various names which in the local toponomy, are given to the streets of Venice. The city is divided into two parts by the Grand Canal which crosses it in the shape of an inverted S. The other canals are called *rii* or *rielli* (rio and riello in the singular) (*rio menuo* is a particularly small rio). There are some 400 bridges crossing them today. The streets are called *calli* or *callette*, or *rughe* when they are lined with houses and shops. *Salizzada* is still used for the first streets to be paved, while some narrow passages are

1) *View of Venice from the south, with St. Mark's dock, and in the foreground, the Basilica della Salute*
2) *San Trovaso "squero" (yard where gondolas are docked, constructed or repaired)*
3) *Rio San Vitale*

still called *stretto*. *Piscina* is a place where there was once a pool of water, *campi* and *campielli* are larger open spaces (also *campazzo*), while *piazza* is only that of San Marco and *piazzetta* that which faces the quay and that next to the Basilica. *Fondamenta* are the streets running along the sides of the rii next to the foundations of the houses. The city is divided into *sentieri*: San Marco, Castello, Cannaregio, S. Croce, S. Polo, Dorsoduro (which includes also the Island of the Giudecca). The toponymy is almost exclusively in the Venetian dialect and uses certain deformations which have become consolidated: Sts. Gervasio and Protasio become St. Trovaso; Sant'Apollinare becomes Sant'Aponal, Sant'Eustachio is transformed into San Stae; portico becomes portego; Ponte delle Meraviglie (Bridge of Marvels) is Ponte dele Maravegie and so on. The Venetian dialect, however, is a living dialect and is spoken by practically all Venetians, a sign that its identity has not yet been overcome by the waves of international tourists. It too is part of that unique urban organism which is Venice, and it too must be saved from the cancellation which other dialects have suffered. Dialect is used also for communication between the gondoliers, those traditional Venetian figures which with their splendid boats represent a spectacle within the spectacle. They row standing up, and with only one oar; at the bends in the canals they call signals in dialect to possible approaching boats. As a rule each gondola is rowed by one gondolier, but

1) *Typical Venetian well-curb*
2) *Rio di San Giovanni*
3) *Ponte delle Turchette*
4-5) *View of Rio della Salute*
6) *Grand Canal and Ponte degli Scalzi*
7) *Grand Canal and Ca' Foscari*
8) *Ponte delle Moravegie*

7 there can, also, be two, one at the bow andone at the stern and they row together sending the gondola silently and smoothly over the water. This very manageable, and in spite of its appearance, very stable craft, is of very ancient origin. In popular touristic iconography the gondola is the emblem of Venice as is the figure of the gondolier. They are an important part of the image of Venice but they also belong to the silence, the acquatic rhythm of Venice, and the «urban music», rich in harmony, which must not be allowed to die.

8

1) Typical view
2) Grand Canal at San Simeon Piccolo
3) Entry of Palazzo Dario
4) Ponte Rialto: the market

Pages 92-93: the Ponte di Rialto at night and its view

1) Arsenal
2) Panorama. In the background: Isola di S. Giorgio
3) Evocative image of high water in Venice
4) Rio della Toletta

1) Evocative view of the Ducal Palace at sunset
2) Gondola on the Grand Canal
3) View of the Ducal Palace and the bell tower
of St. Mark's basilica
4) Dei Carmini school and church
5) New Ghetto
6) Church of the Madonna dell'Orto
7) San Nicolò church

97

Folklore

To the glorious past of the Serenissima, and to its majestic spirit, correspond not only the splendour of its architecture and the richness of its art treasures, but also a tradition for celebrating festivals which today echo the most ancient and numerous *palace feasts* which, at various times of year, filled the canals of the city with colour and music and represented for the Venetians a moment of identification with their city and each other; this seems to have been quite unique to the Republic. Only a few of these feasts are still celebrated today: but on those occasions Venice goes back centuries in its calendar and dresses in the clothes of its ancient moments of glory. The famous *Historic Regatta* is held on the first Sunday in September and is a gigantic rowing race in which pairs of gondoliers race in gondolas from St. Mark's Basin, along the Grand Canal to Piazzale Roma and back to where the new Rio turns into the Canal. The historical regatta takes place on the Grand Canal before the gondola race: enormous and sumptuous versions of the traditional gondola, the *Bissone*, move in procession rowed by oarsmen in eighteenth century costume. Sea gods, sea horses, and mermaids, decorate the boats among gilded fringes and embroideries in a spectacle which has the pomp and fascination of the Siena horse race, which makes it the most spectacular festival of the Summer. The *Feast of the Redeemer* is celebrated on the third Sunday in July, this is a religious festival instituted as a votive offering following the liberation from the plague in 1576. It is still an important festival for Venetians who take part in a solemn procession. Two pontoon bridges are constructed for the occasion to join St. Mark's to the Salute Church and Giudecca Island. Thousands of lights between sea and sky illuminate the paths beside the rafts and one the Giudecca, and the many boats which are decorated for the occasion, making a frame for the festival which tends to become very lively in the evening and ends, between blows and showers of colours, with the fireworks display over the waters of the Lagoon. On Sunday of the *Ascension*, a Spring feast, one of the Republic's most evocative ceremonies at sea is remembered. On that day the Doge used to board the *Bucintoro*, the sumptuous official craft of the dogate and have himself rowed to the Lido port. There he performed «the marriage with the sea»: a ring was thrown into the sea while the Doge pronounced the words «perpetuo dominio». This festival goes back to 1000, the year in which, on Ascension Day, Pietro Orseolo II sent off the army which was to conquer Istria and Dalmatia. For this festival (which Venetians call the Feast of the Sensa), in the days of the Republic Venetian and foreign merchants displayed their merchandise in a spectacular international market in Piazza San Marco and the Piazzetta. Other festivals such as that for the Purification of the Virgin, or for the Madonna of Health, celebrated ancient victories or gave thanks for liberation from the scourge of the plague, and were less elaborate than those we have mentioned. But the famous festival of the Vogalonga (long row) is really more a rite, in which the Venetians reappropriate the sea. This is very close to the daily life and natural relationship of Venice with the sea. On the day of the *Vogalonga* which varies from year to year, thousands of Venetians go into the water in myriads of boats of all types and, starting from St. Mark's Basin, circumnavigate the city and row along the Grand Canal in a joyous festival of rowing, not without some competitive spirit and encouraged and hailed by the crowds along the fondamenta, and at the windows of the houses.

Photographs from page 100 to page 103: the historical regatta. Before the gigantic rowing competition with gondoliers rowing two-oar gondolas, the Historical Regatta takes place on the Grand Canal. The most spectacular moment of the festival is when the entourage of gondolas and "bissone" (large eight-oar Venetian boats), with their sumptuous decorations and 18th century costumes, glide under the Ponte di Rialto. Along the banks of the canal, among the splendid old palaces reflected in the water, time truly seems to have been turned back several centuries.

The more «terrestrial» festival is Carnival which has returned to popularity again in recent years to a point where the city literally gets invaded by tourists from all over Italy and from abroad. This festival, of ancient Greek and Roman origins, is celebrated during the period which in the Catholic-Christian lithurgical calendar falls between Epiphany and Lent. The name carnival probably comes from the instruction to avoid eating meats (car-nem levare in Latin) during Lent. And carnival, preceding the renunciation of meat, became a period of feasting and unruliness celebrated, principally on Fat Tuesday and Thursday, by amusements and the joys of the palate. And the amusement, as in the Latin Saturnalia, consisted mainly in breaking the rules of society, in ignoring the rules which regulated the relationship between the different social classes, and in the general release from work and worry which filled every-day life. In this context, the carnival masks and costumes become a means of exchanging one's identity with that of another and playing a new role. Thus Venice becomes a vast stage for an immense, mobile, multicoloured

Photographs from page 104-107: scenes from the Venetian Carnival.
For a few days life in Venice becomes a spectacle and festival. With Carnival characterized by the breaking of social rules, the masks become a way to change one's identity. Venice transforms into a brightly colored stage for thousands of costumes, each more fantastic than the next. Concerts and dances take place on St. Mark's square, and the festival ends with the burning of the Old Lady, a propitiatory ritual to renew natural energies.

theatrical show, where thousands of people in masks compete with each other for the eccentricity and phantasy of their costumes: some from the comedy of arts like Harlequin, Punch, Columbine, Pantaloon - made famous by Goldoni's comedies - and those of ancient Doges and military leaders of the Serenissima, and others from the rich society of eighteenth century Venice; all the way to completely imaginary creations with thousands of variations. At the time of the Republic the carnival festival reached its height on fat Thursday in memory of the victory over Ulric, Patriarch of Aquileia, who was condemned to donate a bull and twelve pigs, an irreverent and insulting symbol referring to the Patriarch and his Canons, to the Doge every year thereafter. The feast culminated on fat Thursday with the killing of the animals by hand by the chief butcher in the courtyard of the Doge's Palace. Other parts of the day's entertainments were represented by the *Moresca*, fencing in the Saracen way, and the descent of the Turk, in which a young acrobat, while he was descending a rope stretched from the bell tower of St. Mark's to the loggia of the Doge's Palace, offered flowers and poems to the Doge.

The Islands

Immediately after leaving the city, with its pulsing life in movement along the canals, and going towards the open sea, the fascinating landscape of the Lagoon is revealed in all its majesty. The two coastal islands of the Lido and Pellestrina separate the Lagoon from the Adriatic, sheltering the over 500 square kilometres of smooth water from the sea. This extraordinary sheet of water always looks the same but in reality is always changing; the play of the tide hides and reveals land at water level, floods and washes valleys and marshes, laps at myriads of large and small islands. A visit to the principal islands is a must. They are reached via canals, a submerged network of waterways marked by poles protruding from the water. And according to their present use and the history of each one, one passes by abandoned islands, and lands at others scintillating with colour and life, and others agains, melancholy monuments or smiling and peaceful centres of prayer, in an atmosphere which changes continually between sea and sky. Torcello has a particular enchantment of its own as it rises out of the calm silence of the lagoon. The elegant and unexpected profile of its beautiful churches can be seen from some distance away. This island, with its gentle melancholy air was inhabited in 452 by the first refugees from Altino in search of shelter from the Barbarian invasions. About a century later the last of the people of Altino fleeing from their devastated city, arrived here with their bishop and Torcello became the episcopal see and administrative centre of the Lagoon community which was the original nucleus of Venice. But the episcopal see was transferred to Burano in the eighteenth century and Torcello went into a decline. Compared with its one time 20,000 inhabitants, only a few tens of persons live on the island today. The principal monuments are grouped as in a theatrical scene around the grass-covered central piazzetta: the Cathedral, the Church of Santa Fosca, the Palace of the Council and the Palace of the Archives. The Cathedral, dedicated to the Assumption, is the most outstanding example of Ravennate architecture in existence in the whole Lagoon. Founded in 639 and enlarged in 864, it was then rebuilt in 1008 and has a Veneto-Byzantine appearance today. Little remains of the octagonal Baptistery opposite the façade of the Cathedral. In the interior, divided into nave and two aisles by columns with Corinthian capitals, the mosaic decorations are the most important and precious aspect. They bear some similarity to the mosaics in St. Mark's and to the older ones in Ravenna. The inner wall of the façade is covered entirely by the very famous *Last Judgement*, a splendid Veneto-Byzantine mosaic of the XII - XIII century. The various pictures following Byzantine iconography include *Christ on the Cross between the Madonna and St. John*, the *Descent into Hell*, the *Deesis* (Christ in Glory) *with the Madonna and St. John the Baptist*, the *12 Apostles*, *Saints and Angels*; the *preparation of the Last Judgement* between two scenes of the *Resurrection Of the Body*; *The Elect* and *The Damned*. In the *presbytery*, a XIII century mosaic depicts the *Annunciation*. The mosaic masterpiece of the Venetian school which represents *The Madonna and the Child giving a Blessing* goes back to the beginning of the same century. Another noteworthy mosaic is that on the cross-vault which precedes the apse representing *Four Angels holding the Mystic Lamb* (XII-XIII cent.), a theme also to be found in San Vitale in Ravenna. Next to the Cathedral, the Church of Santa Fosca, on a central plan, over-looks the main piazzetta of Torcello. It has a pleasing, harmoniously proportioned interior and is surrounded on five sides by an arcade of arches on columns with Veneto-Byzantine capitals. A beautiful basrelief of the fifteenth century in the right hand side of the church depicts *Santa Fosca Venerated by her Colleagues*. The Palace of the Archives and the Palace of the Council are situated in front of the Basilica and Santa Fosca Church, they both date from the fourteenth century and both now house the Estuary Museum which contains archaeological remains from various sources and of varying historical significance regarding the Lagoon culture.

Island of San Giorgio

Away from the piazzetta which is its heart, the rest of the island has few houses and fewer restaurants, but for this very reason offers an opportunity for a delightful, quiet walk in picturesque surroundings practically undisturbed by domestic noises. Murano is quite different, lively and populous on its five small islands which are still the active centre of the famous glass craft industry. All the Venetian glass furnaces were moved here in 1292 to avoid the danger from possible fires. The art of glass making is very ancient and is allied to the art of mosaic with its Ravennate and Byzantine origins, in which the Venetians excel. The Museum of Glass in Murano contains a magnificent collection of specimens of this highly refined art which in the sixteenth and eighteenth centuries had its golden periods with the establishment of the illustrious, Barovier, Ballarin, Seguso and Toso families besides others, the true aristocrats of glasswork. (This art was so highly regarded that the daughters of glassworkers married into the nobility and became patricians). Besides blown, white, coloured, engraved, and cold painted glass, Murano had and still has, not only the original glass production but also that of paste in coloured glass often imitating hard stones, used for costume jewellery and necklaces.

TORCELLO
1) Torcello: detail of the courtyard in front of the baptistery
2) Torcello: the throne of Attila in the grassy square
3) Aerial view of the Basilica
4) Well-curb
5) Roman ruins

4

5

TORCELLO

1) View of the right nave in the Torcello basilica

2) Detail of the iconostasis - 14th-15th century

3) Detail of the central apse: the Benedictory Virgin with Child

4) The "Pluteo dei Pavoni." Venetian-Byzantine relief from the 11th century

113

TORCELLO
1) The great mosaic of the Last Judgment
2) Detail of the central apse: the six Apostles on the right side
3) Detail of the central apse: the six Apostles on the left side

Page 116-117: the Torcello "square"

The glassworks still produce all the traditional glass objects and also pursue an aesthetic and formal research which results in an artistic production of high quality. The numerous laboratories and workshops allow visitors to watch the pieces being made, blown and finished before their eyes. But the island has not produced only master glass workers. It was also the native land of the Vivarini family who were among the most illustrious painter of the Venetian school. Murano, a very lively centre in the past, was at the height of its splendour in the sixteenth century when rich Venetians, artists and writers used to spend their holidays there: it had palaces, villas, churches, monasteries, and 30,000 inhabitants which made Murano into a second, little Venice. Even today though it has lost its sixteenth century splendour it is still a pleasant and attractive centre. Among the most interesting of the old buildings, there is the Church of St. Peter the Martyr which dates from 1348 but has been almost entirely rebuilt. Constructed in brick, the church has a façade with a Renaissance doorway while the sides are decorated with Romanesque motives. A portico of sixteenth century arches at the side of the church is all that remains of the ancient cloister.

MURANO
1) Aerial view of Murano
2, 3, 4, 5) Glassworks in Murano: glass art, which continued that from Roman times, has made the island famous worldwide.

MURANO
1) *View of the central nave of the Church of*
S.S. Maria e Donato
2) *Outside view of the apse*
3) *Mosaic floor from 1140*

Burano strikes one from a distance for the brilliance of its colours. This, also founded by refugees from Altino, occupies 4 small islands and is built modestly but with considerable charm. Small multicoloured houses line the principal canals and miniscule calli, between lines of washing, fish markets and open thresholds in a wonderful game in which the border between private and public property completely disappears and life goes on in an atmosphere of friendly domesticity. Then, suddenly, we meet the *lace*; sometimes it is being made in the open doorway of a house where the woman can also keep an eye on the children playing in the campiello, but it is also on display for sale in the little craft shops. Lace is everywhere, mostly white, intricate and precious, and waving in the breeze like so many flags on the stalls against the pastel coloured background of the houses. This anonymous form of feminine art for which Burano is famous, reaches heights of real virtuosity. It became popular in the sixteenth century and was cultivated by the Doganessas Giovanna Duodo and Morosina Morosini, the wives respectively of Pasquale Malipiero and Marino Grimani. A last unusual touch is given to the island by the bell tower of the Parish Church of St. Martin in Piazza Galuppi which, with a considerable list, rises above the rooftops.

BURANO

1) Burano: the unmistakable crooked bell tower is a constant presence on the horizon
2, 3, 4) The art of lace-making, which seemed to have disappeared, has been recovered, and today the skilled hands of women weave delicate embroidery in air stitch, rosette stitch and open work.
5) Overlooking the Palazzo del Podestà is the Piazza Galluppi, where the lace-making school, now a museum, was located.

Not far from Burano, the tiny island of St. Francis of the Desert evocative and solitary, is the home of a Franciscan Convent. The island was donated to the Franciscan Order in 1228 by Jacopo Michiel. It is said that St. Francis rested there on his return from the Middle East and in recognition of this episode the island was given to the Minor Friars. It is possible to stop here, visit the little church which has two cloister and, among tall cypress trees, the lovely secluded garden cared for by the Brothers. From the Minor Father's beautiful garden one's gaze wanders slowly over the spectacle of the Lagoon and the lazy coming and going of the boats floating on the water.

ST. FRANCIS OF THE DESERT
1) The rays of the setting sun are reflected in the warm water
2) Shoals and reeds as far as the eye can see
3) St. Francis: the cross of Christ stands out against the terra-cotta
4) St. Francis of the Desert: view of Burano and the northern lagoon
5) Façade of the St. Francis church with its lovely pointed bell tower
6) The bare interior of the church

4

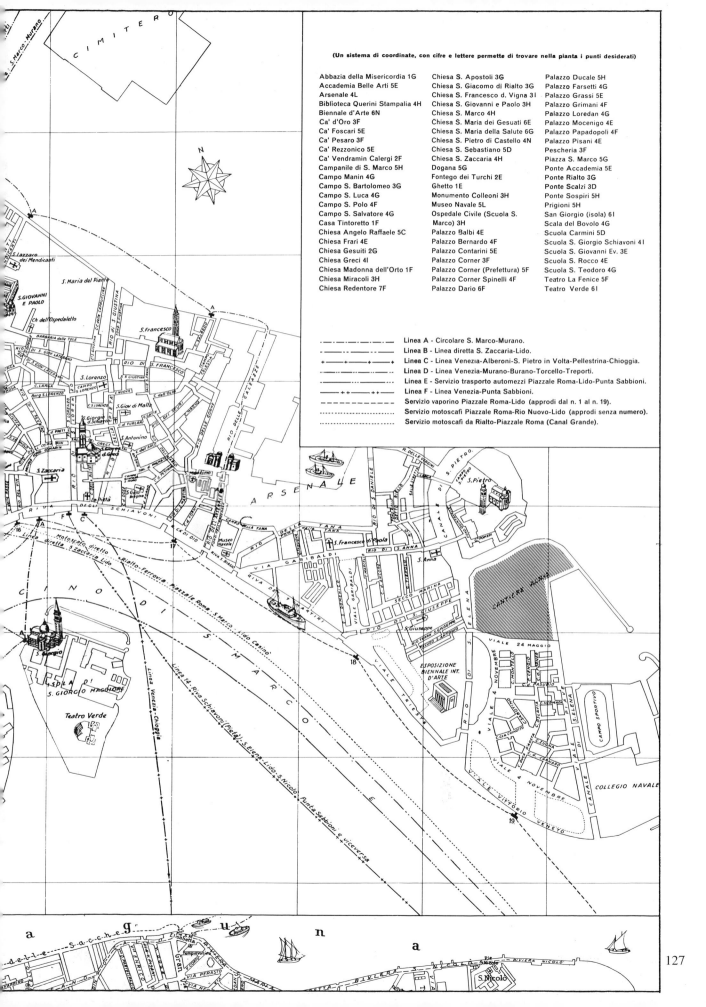

Linea A - Circolare S. Marco-Murano.
Linea B - Linea diretta S. Zaccaria-Lido.
Linea C - Linea Venezia-Alberoni-S. Pietro in Volta-Pellestrina-Chioggia.
Linea D - Linea Venezia-Murano-Burano-Torcello-Treporti.
Linea E - Servizio trasporto automezzi Piazzale Roma-Lido-Punta Sabbioni.
Linea F - Linea Venezia-Punta Sabbioni.
Servizio vaporino Piazzale Roma-Lido (approdi dal n. 1 al n. 19).
Servizio motoscafi Piazzale Roma-Rio Nuovo-Lido (approdi senza numero).
Servizio motoscafi da Rialto-Piazzale Roma (Canal Grande).

INDEX